Good Dog, Bad Breath

by Mike Peters

TOR®

A TOM DOHERTY ASSOCIATES BOOK
NEW YORK

This is a work of fiction. All the characters and events portrayed in this book are either products of the author's imagination or are used fictitiously.

GRIMMY™: GOOD DOG, BAD BREATH

http://www.grimmy.com

This book contains material published previously in a trade edition as *Grimmy: The Postman Always Screams Twice.*

A Tor Book
Published by Tom Doherty Associates, Inc.
175 Fifth Avenue
New York, NY 10010

Tor Books on the World Wide Web:
http://www.tor.com

Tor® is a registered trademark of Tom Doherty Associates, Inc.

ISBN: 0-812-59090-2

First edition: February 1996
First mass market edition: February 1999

Printed in the United States of America

0 9 8 7 6 5 4 3 2 1

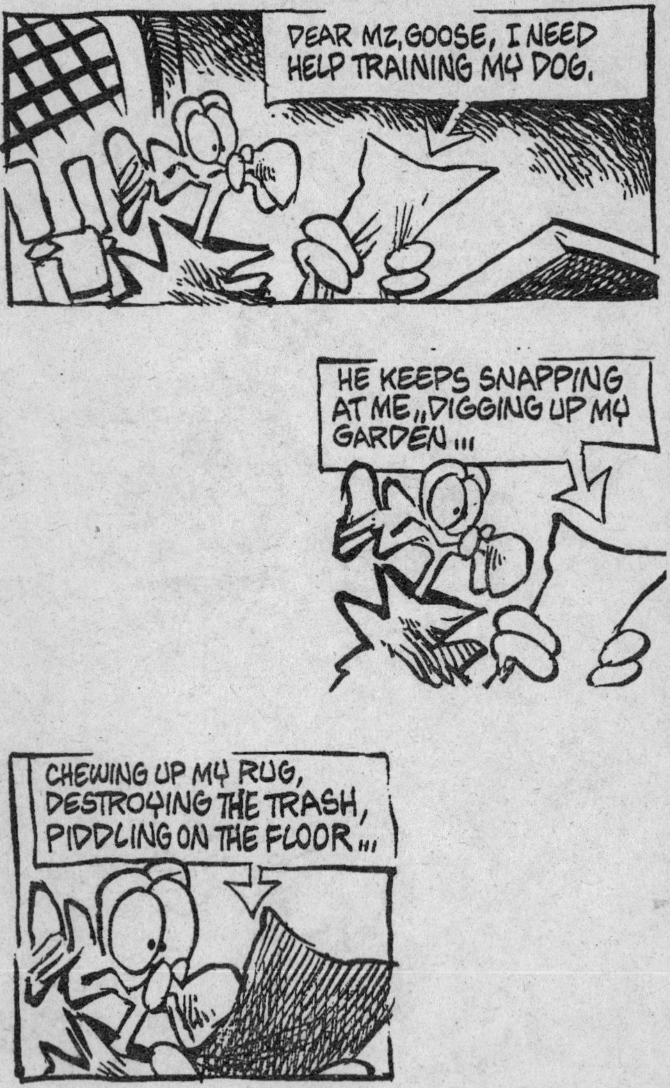
DEAR MZ, GOOSE, I NEED HELP TRAINING MY DOG.
HE KEEPS SNAPPING AT ME,, DIGGING UP MY GARDEN...
CHEWING UP MY RUG, DESTROYING THE TRASH, PIDDLING ON THE FLOOR...

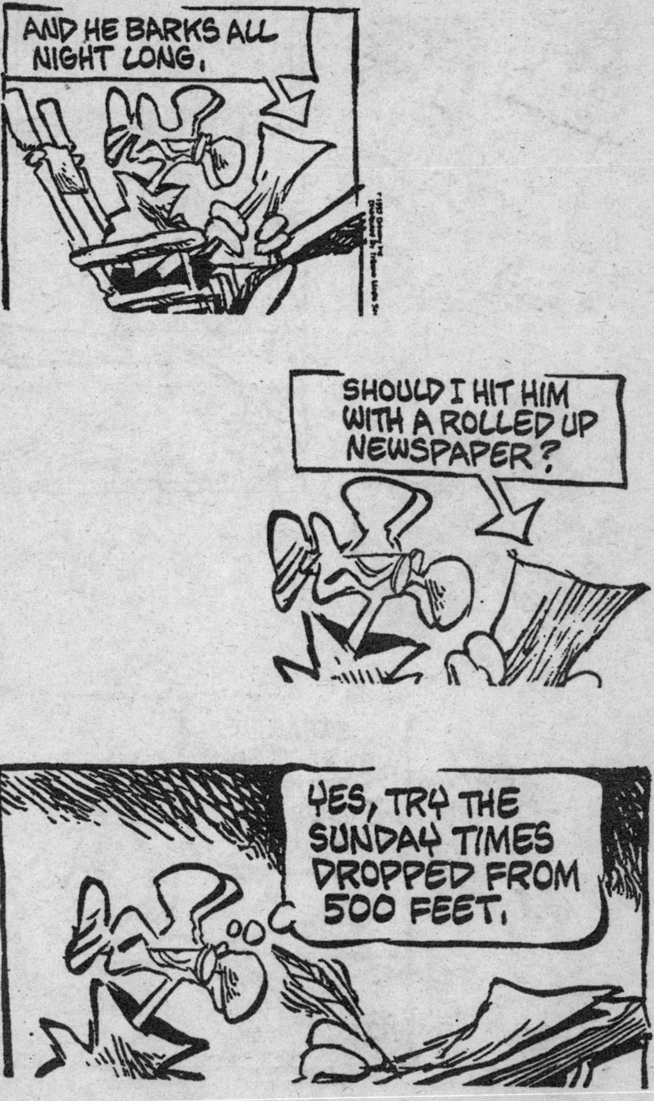

AND HE BARKS ALL NIGHT LONG.
SHOULD I HIT HIM WITH A ROLLED UP NEWSPAPER?
YES, TRY THE SUNDAY TIMES DROPPED FROM 500 FEET.

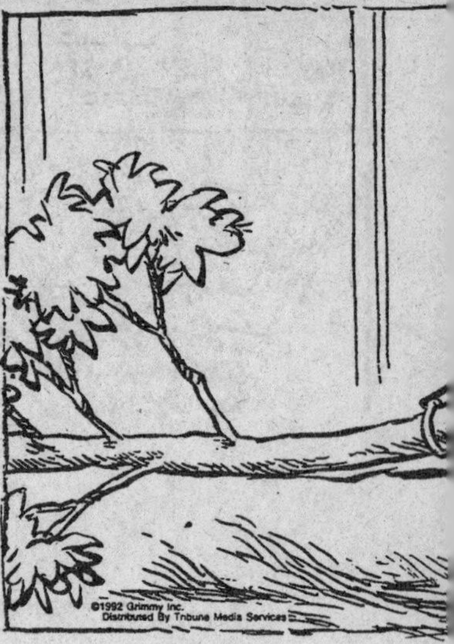
©1992 Grimmy Inc.
Distributed By Tribune Media Services

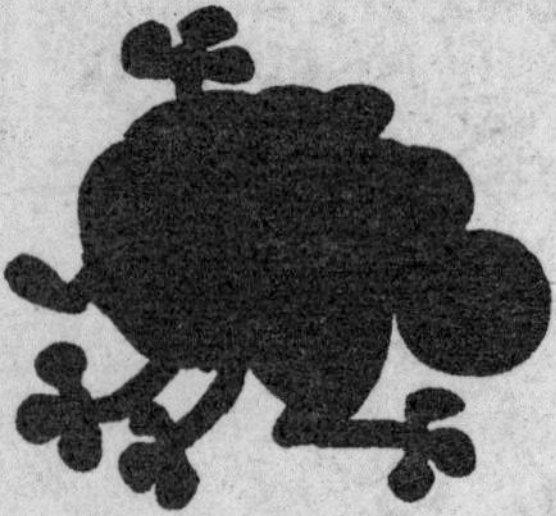

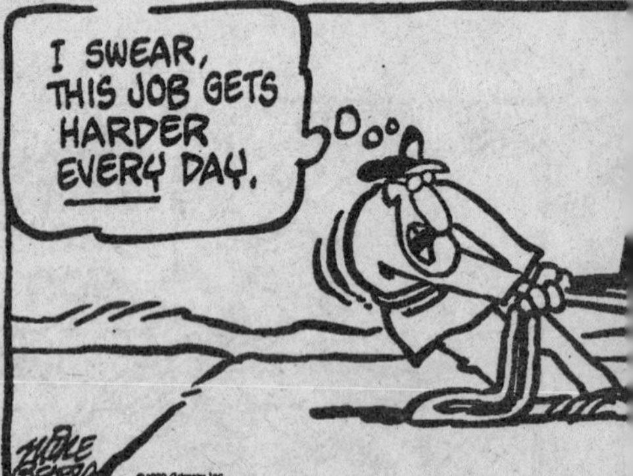
I SWEAR, THIS JOB GETS HARDER EVERY DAY.
MIKE PETERS

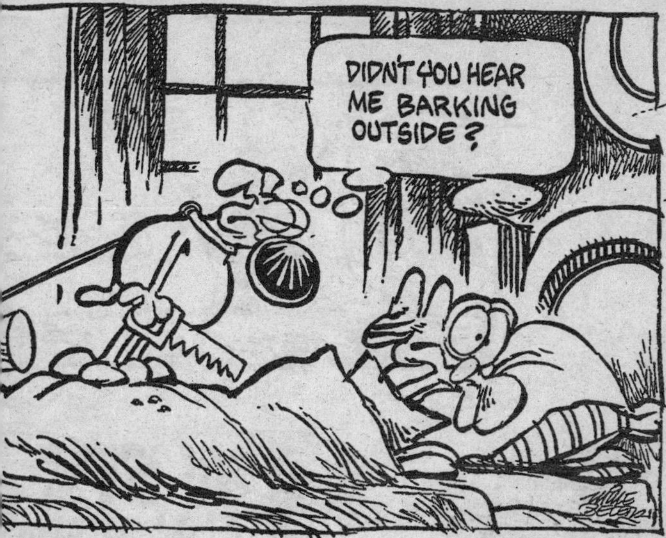
DIDN'T YOU HEAR ME BARKING OUTSIDE?

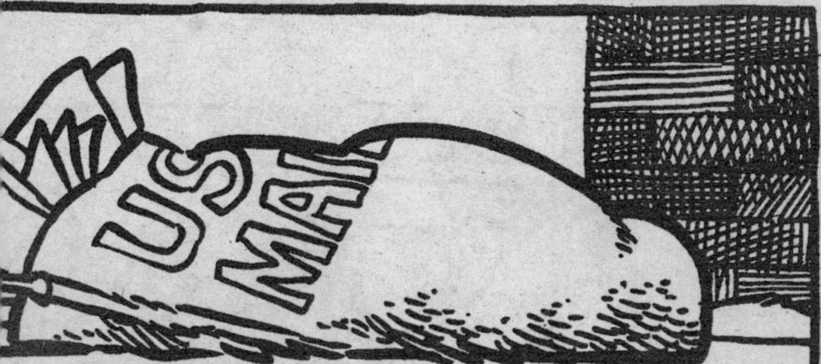
US
MAI

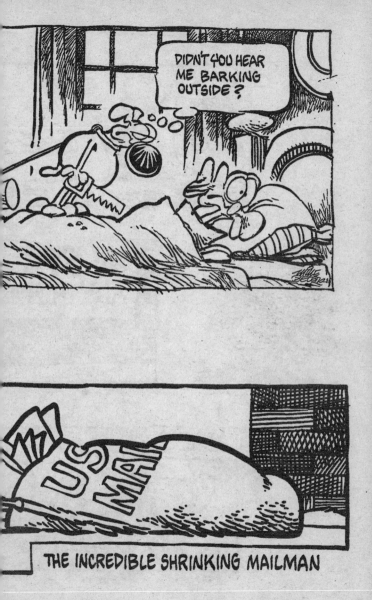

THE INCREDIBLE SHRINKING MAILMAN

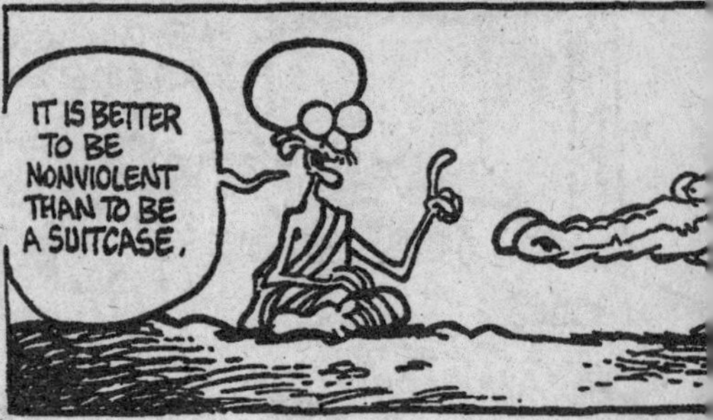
IT IS BETTER TO BE NONVIOLENT THAN TO BE A SUITCASE.

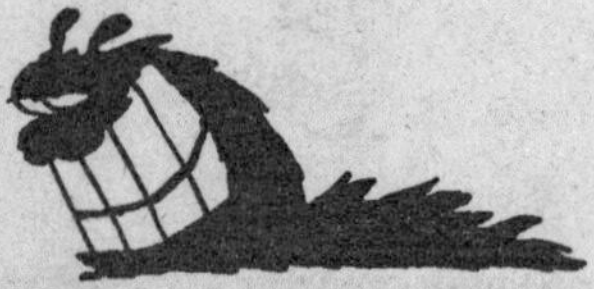

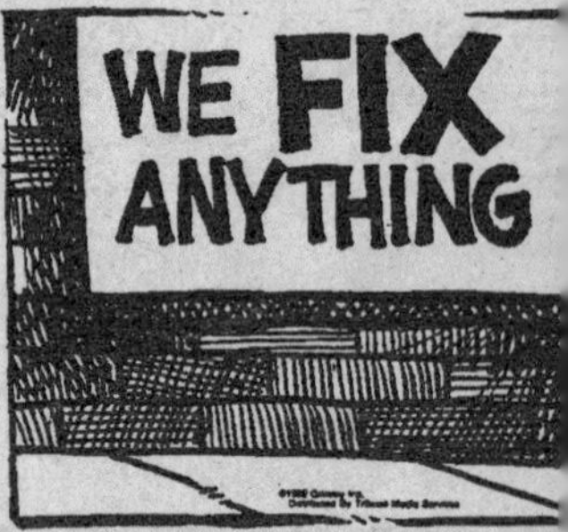
WE FIX ANYTHING

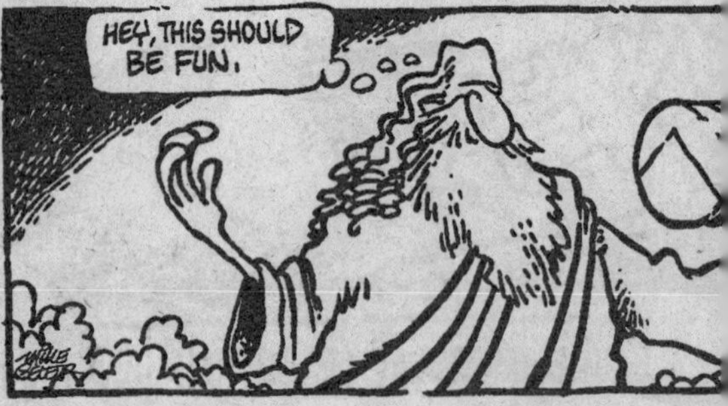
HEY, THIS SHOULD BE FUN.

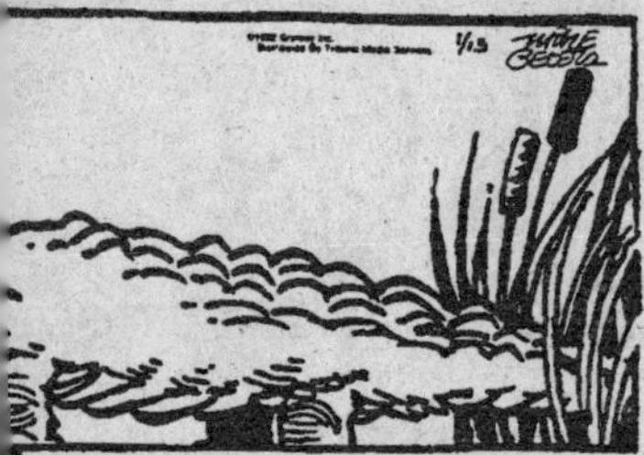

CROCODILE GANDHI

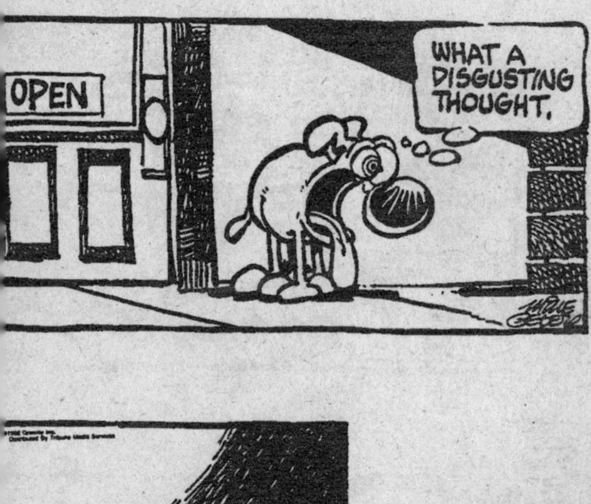
OPEN
WHAT A DISGUSTING THOUGHT.

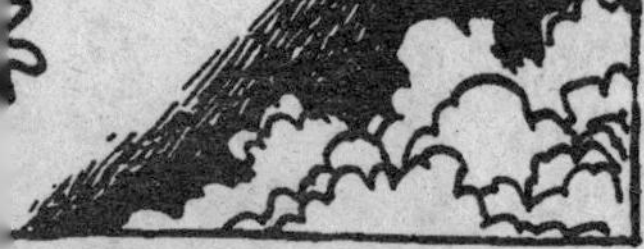

THE TRUTH BEHIND THE BIG BANG THEORY

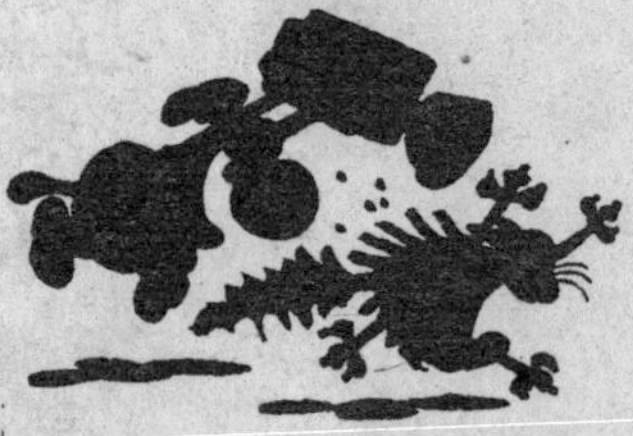

BUG ACTING CLASS

YES, YES... I SEE YOU IN A FANCY RESTAURANT, SURROUNDED BY EGGS BENEDICT AND ENGLISH MUFFINS...

WHOA... WHAT'S A JOINT LIKE THIS DOING IN A GIRL LIKE YOU?

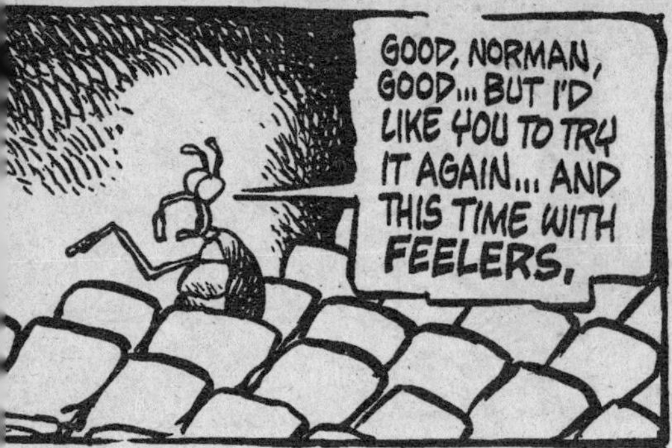
GOOD, NORMAN, GOOD... BUT I'D LIKE YOU TO TRY IT AGAIN... AND THIS TIME WITH FEELERS.

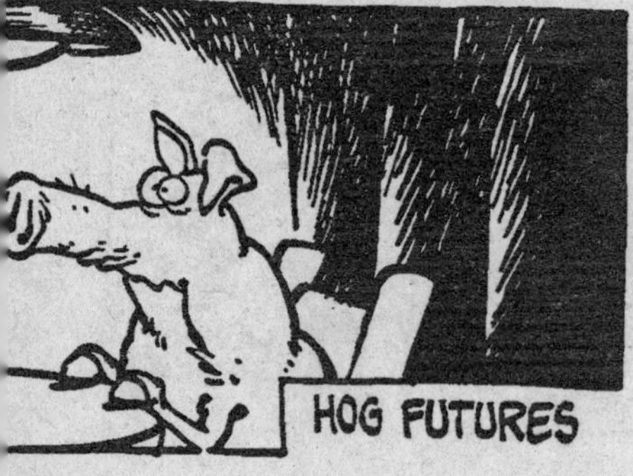
HOG FUTURES

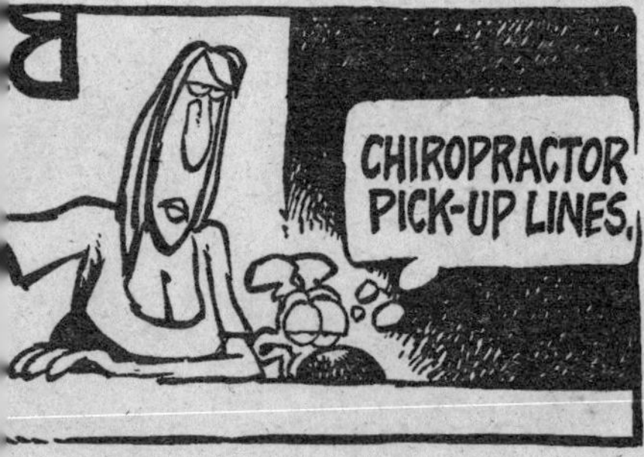
CHIROPRACTOR PICK-UP LINES.

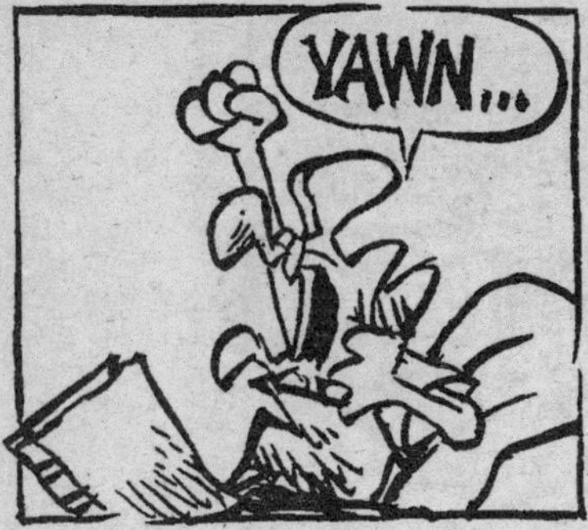
YAWN...

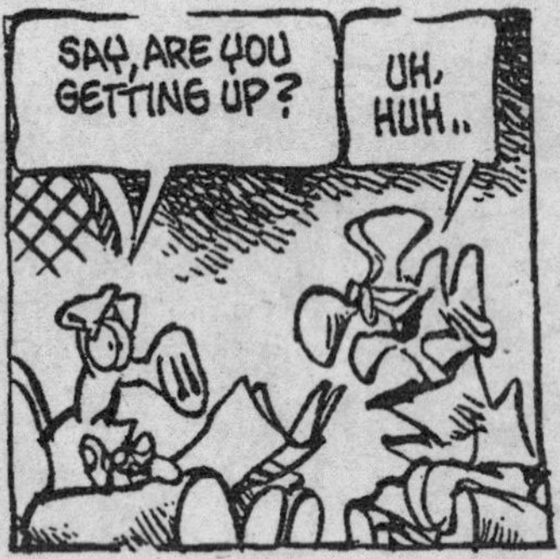
SAY, ARE YOU GETTING UP?
UH, HUH..

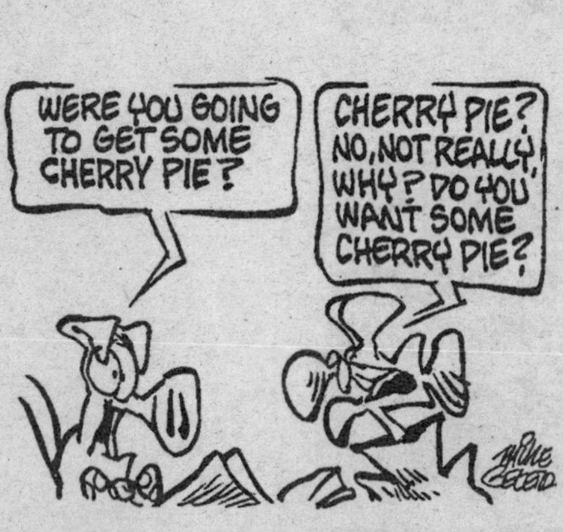
WERE YOU GOING TO GET SOME CHERRY PIE?
CHERRY PIE? NO, NOT REALLY, WHY? DO YOU WANT SOME CHERRY PIE?

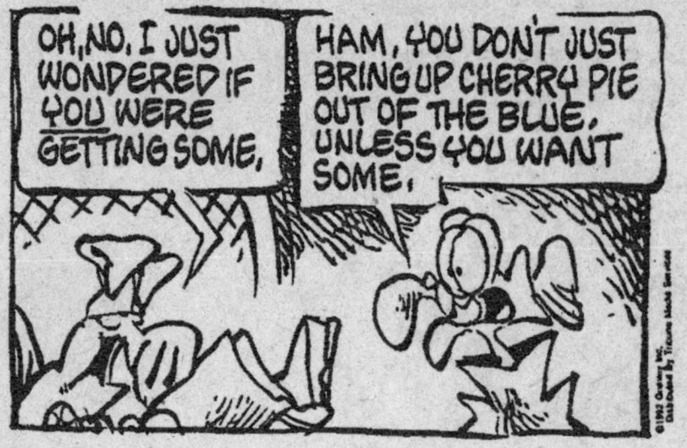
OH, NO. I JUST WONDERED IF YOU WERE GETTING SOME.
HAM, YOU DON'T JUST BRING UP CHERRY PIE OUT OF THE BLUE. UNLESS YOU WANT SOME.

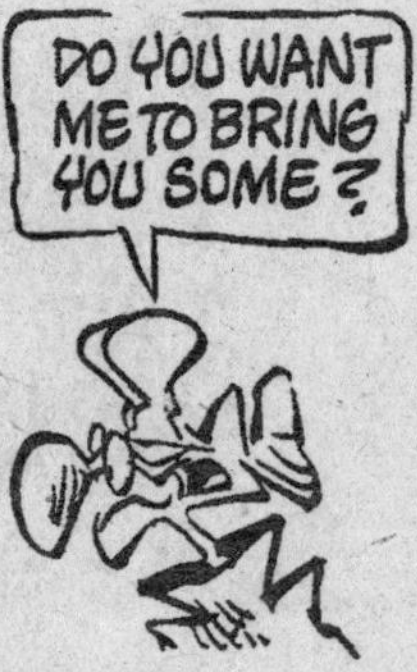
DO YOU WANT ME TO BRING YOU SOME?

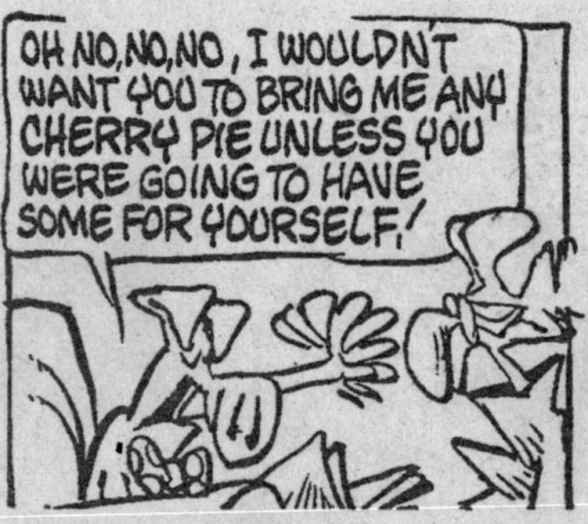
OH NO, NO, NO, I WOULDN'T WANT YOU TO BRING ME ANY CHERRY PIE UNLESS YOU WERE GOING TO HAVE SOME FOR YOURSELF!

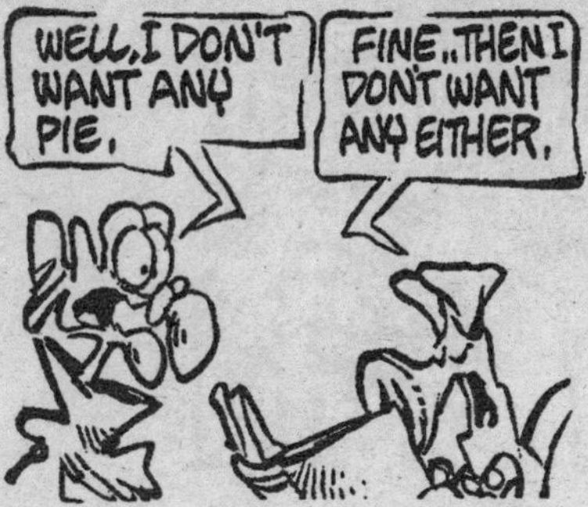
WELL, I DON'T WANT ANY PIE.
FINE.. THEN I DON'T WANT ANY EITHER.

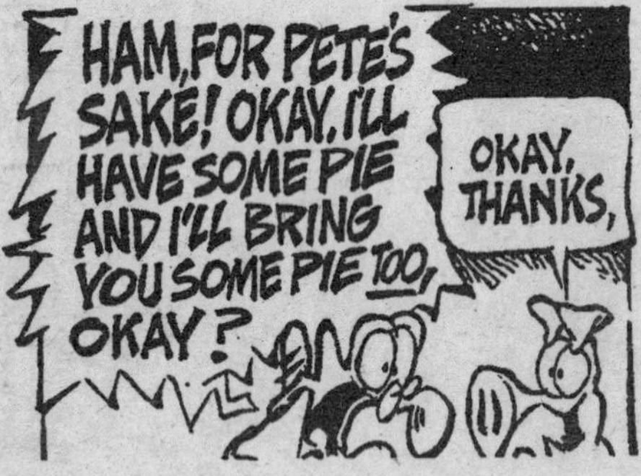
HAM, FOR PETE'S SAKE! OKAY, I'LL HAVE SOME PIE AND I'LL BRING YOU SOME PIE TOO, OKAY?
OKAY, THANKS.

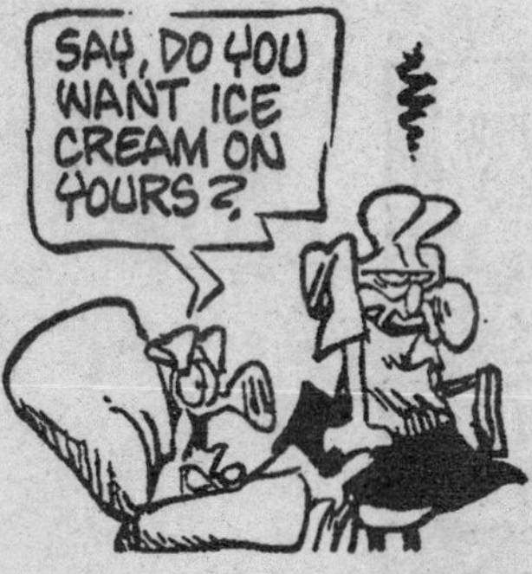
SAY, DO YOU WANT ICE CREAM ON YOURS?

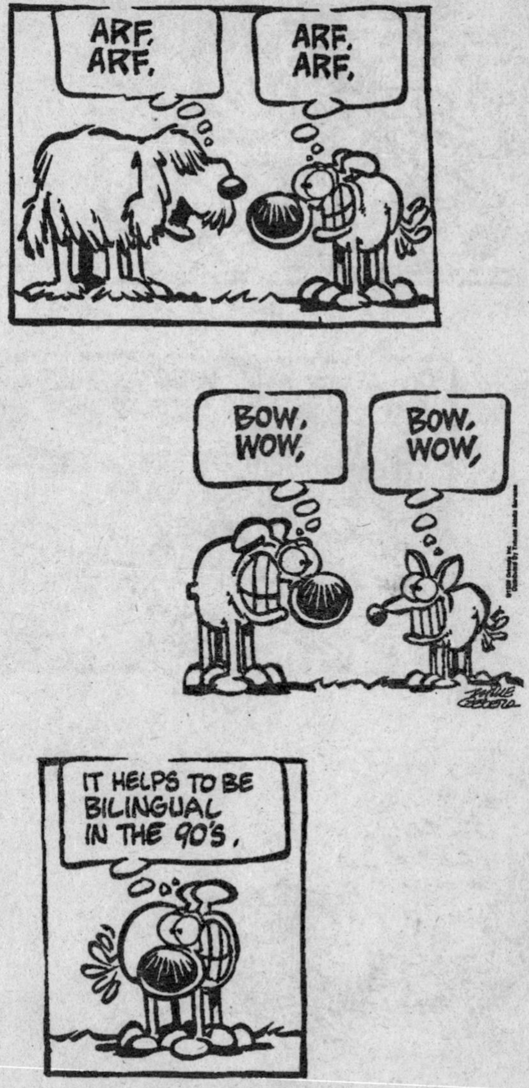

ARF. ARF.
ARF. ARF.
BOW. WOW.
BOW. WOW.
IT HELPS TO BE BILINGUAL IN THE 90'S.

HERE, GRIMMY, IT'S RAINING. YOU USE THE UMBRELLA.

YOU PAMPER HIM TOO MUCH.
HAVE YOU EVER SMELLED WET DOG?

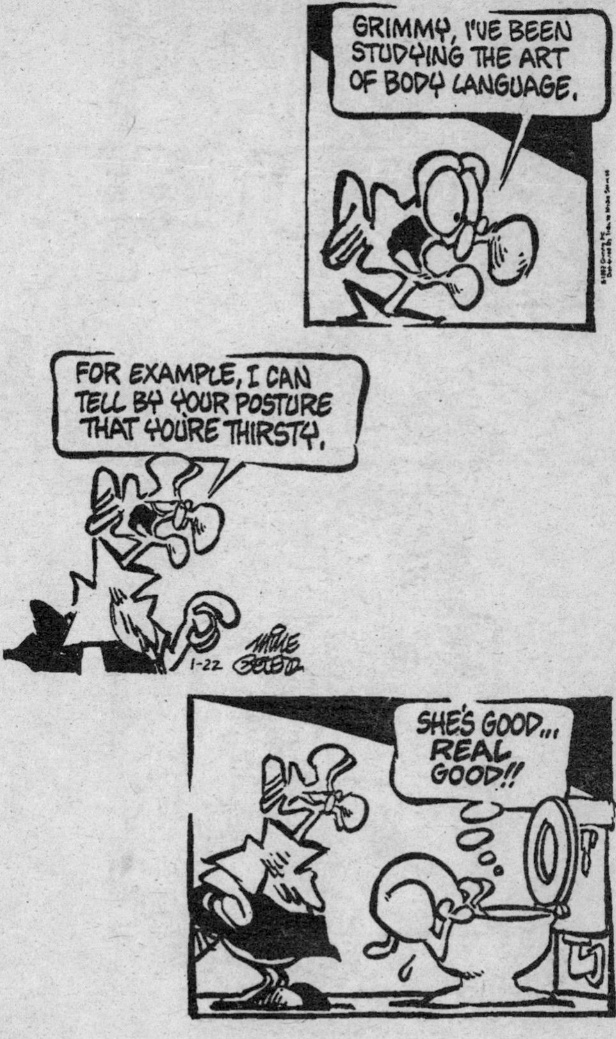
GRIMMY, I'VE BEEN STUDYING THE ART OF BODY LANGUAGE.
FOR EXAMPLE, I CAN TELL BY YOUR POSTURE THAT YOU'RE THIRSTY.
1-22
SHE'S GOOD... REAL GOOD!!

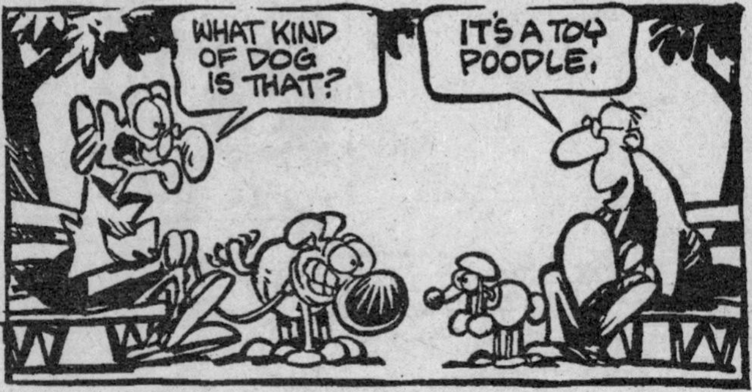
WHAT KIND OF DOG IS THAT?
IT'S A TOY POODLE.

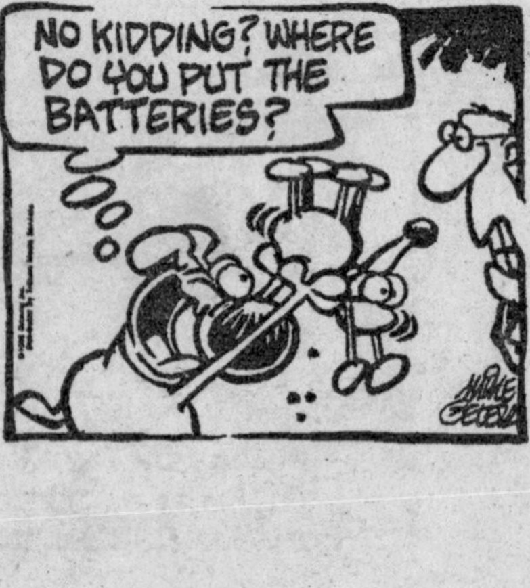
NO KIDDING? WHERE DO YOU PUT THE BATTERIES?

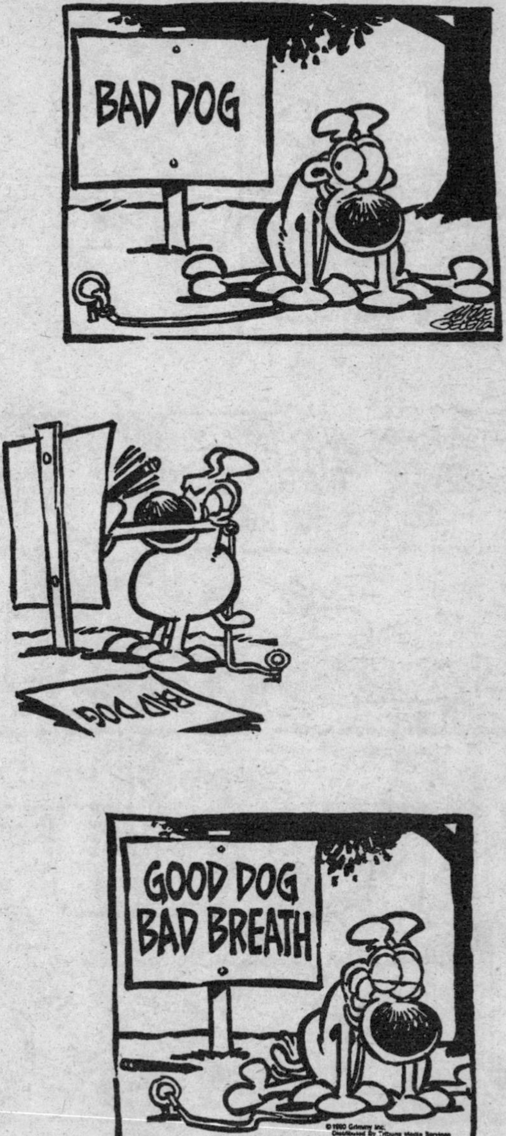
BAD DOG
BAD DOG
GOOD DOG
BAD BREATH

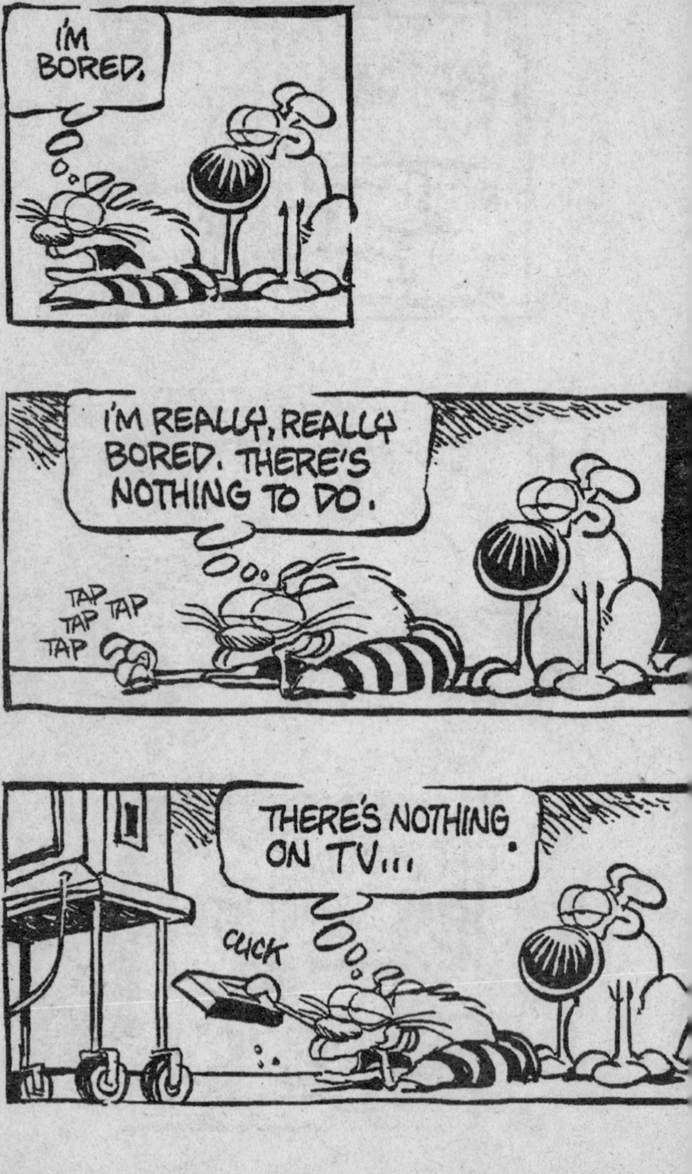
I'M BORED.
I'M REALLY, REALLY BORED. THERE'S NOTHING TO DO.
TAP TAP TAP TAP
THERE'S NOTHING ON TV...
CLICK

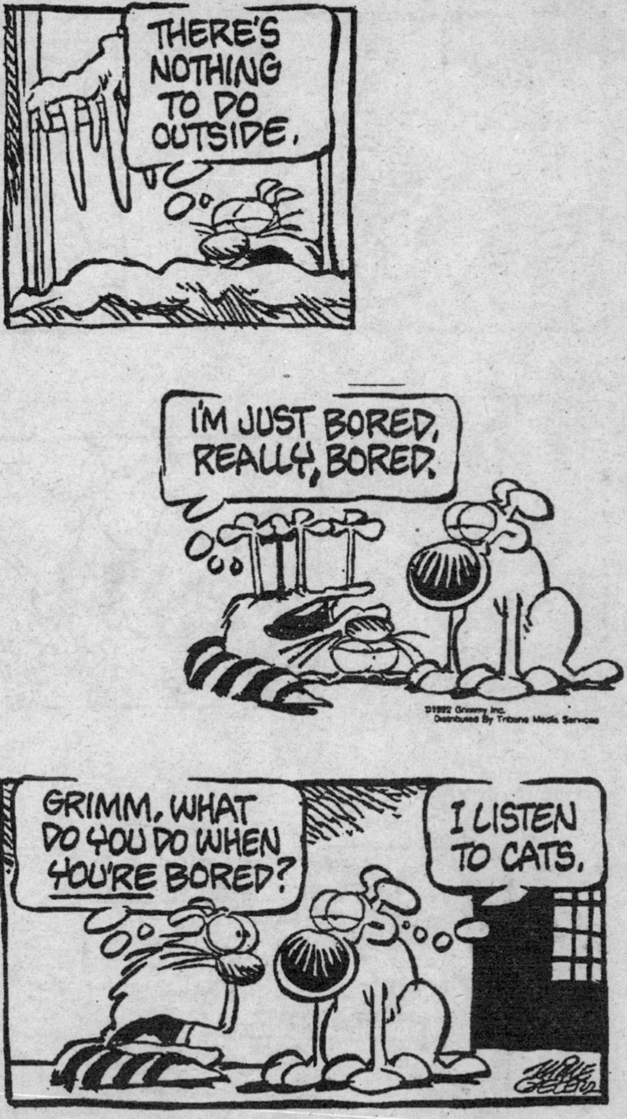
THERE'S NOTHING TO DO OUTSIDE.
I'M JUST BORED, REALLY, BORED.
©1992 Grimmy Inc.
Distributed By Tribune Media Services
GRIMM, WHAT DO YOU DO WHEN YOU'RE BORED?
I LISTEN TO CATS.

A CORPSE IS A CORPSE, OF COURSE, OF COURSE, AND NO ONE WOULD TALK TO A CORPSE, OF COURSE, THAT IS, OF COURSE, UNLESS THE CORPSE, IS THE FAMOUS MR. DEAD...

I LOVE DANCING, BUT I REALLY SHOULD TAKE TIME TO FLOSS.

FRED ASTAIRE AND GINGIVITIS

IT'S WORKING, IT'S WORKING,

DUCK BLIND

TAP TAP TAP...

1-24

OMBIE SITCOMS

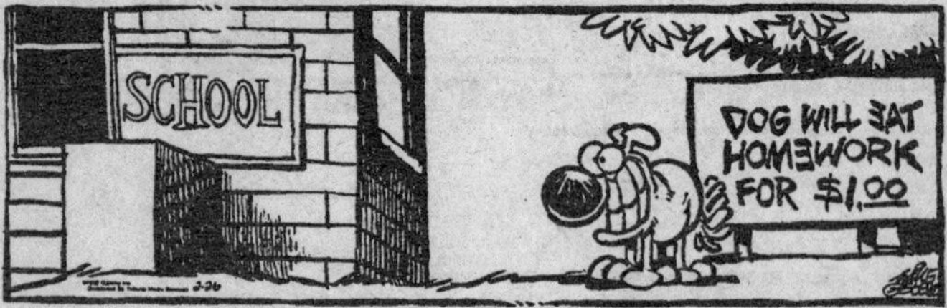
SCHOOL
DOG WILL EAT HOMEWORK FOR $1.00

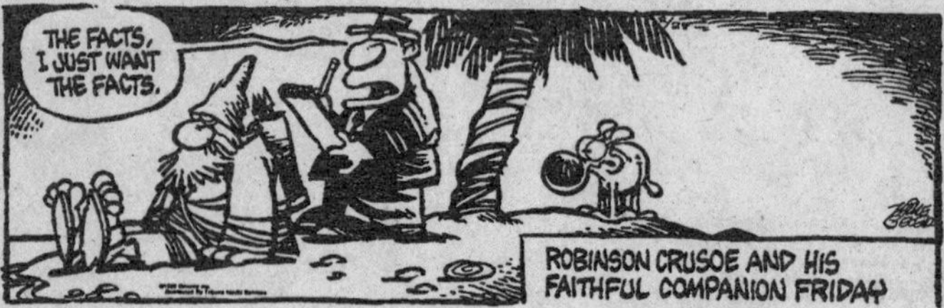
THE FACTS, I JUST WANT THE FACTS.
ROBINSON CRUSOE AND HIS FAITHFUL COMPANION FRIDAY

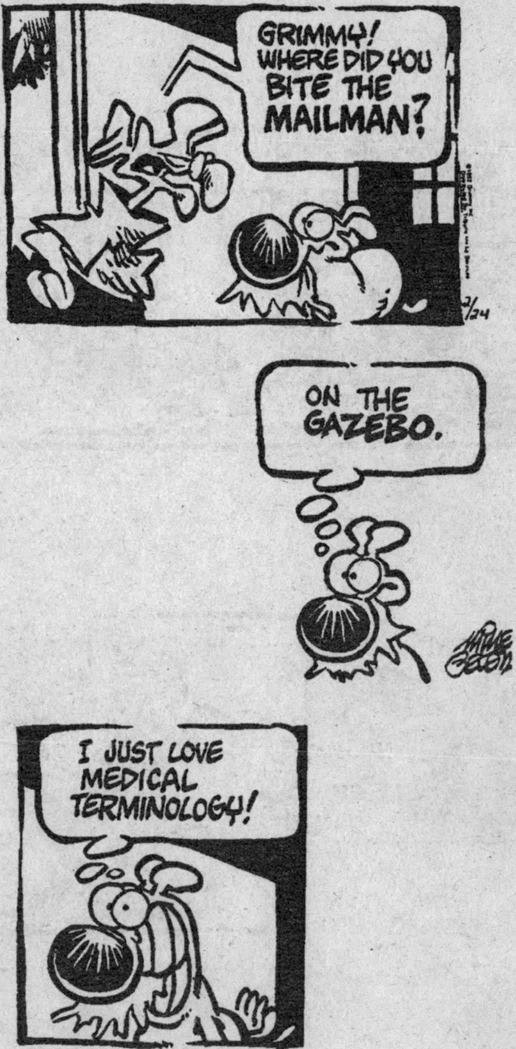
GRIMMY! WHERE DID YOU BITE THE MAILMAN?
2/24
ON THE GAZEBO.
I JUST LOVE MEDICAL TERMINOLOGY!

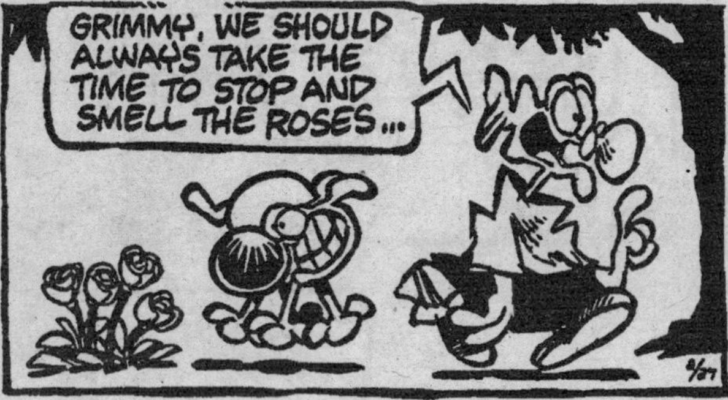
GRIMMY, WE SHOULD ALWAYS TAKE THE TIME TO STOP AND SMELL THE ROSES...

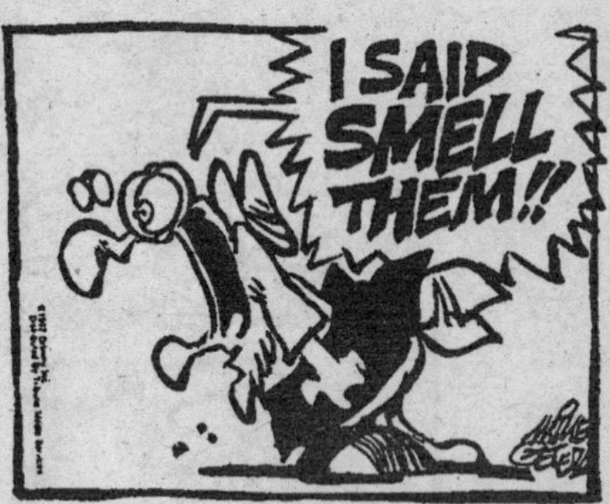
I SAID SMELL THEM!!

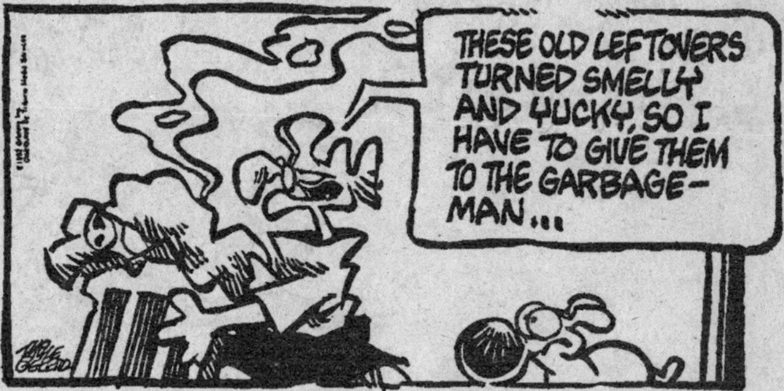
THESE OLD LEFTOVERS TURNED SMELLY AND YUCKY, SO I HAVE TO GIVE THEM TO THE GARBAGE-MAN...

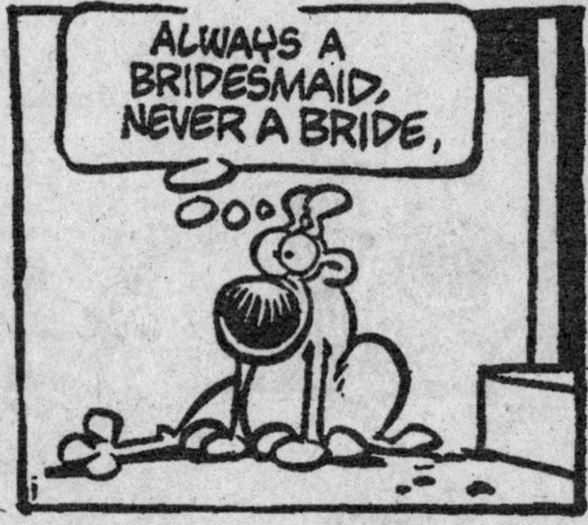
ALWAYS A BRIDESMAID, NEVER A BRIDE,

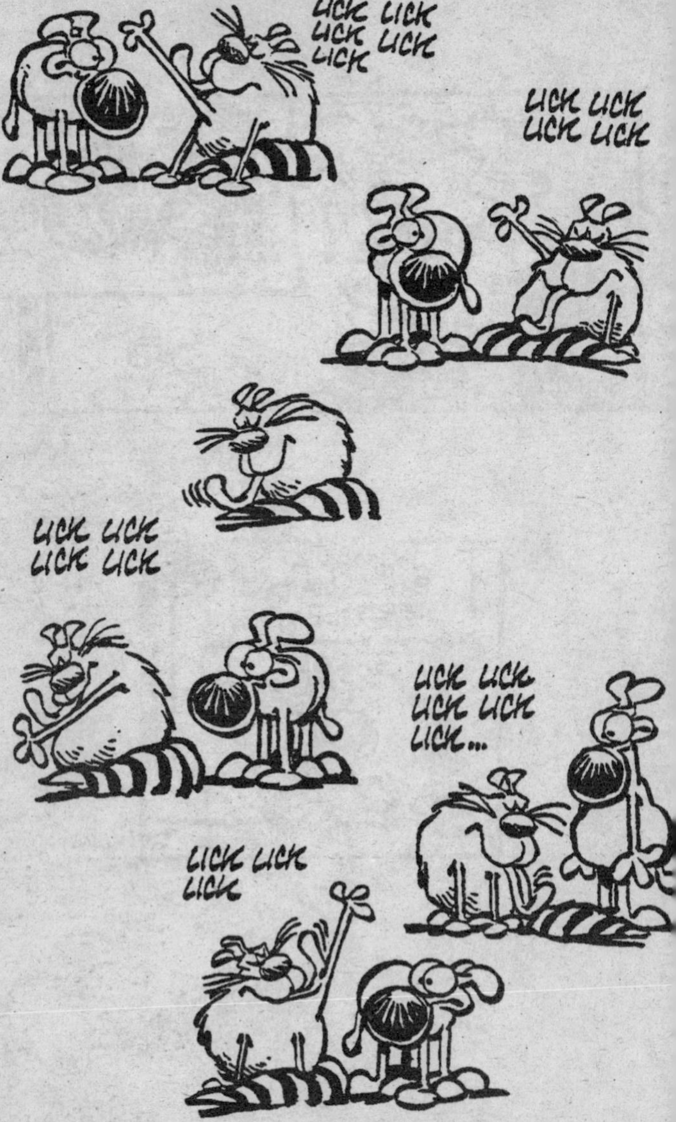
LICK LICK
LICK LICK
LICK
LICK LICK
LICK LICK
LICK LICK
LICK LICK
LICK LICK
LICK LICK
LICK...
LICK LICK
LICK

SORRY.. I CAN'T GO OUT TONIGHT, I'M DEAD....I'M REALLY DEAD.

GENERAL PATTON →

BACK FROM YOUR DATE, YOUNG LADY? I HOPE THAT'S A BLOODSUCKING MARK ON YOUR NECK AND NOT A **HICKEY**...

WHY ZOMBIES DON'T DATE MUCH

COLONEL
ORTH

MAJOR
WEDGEY

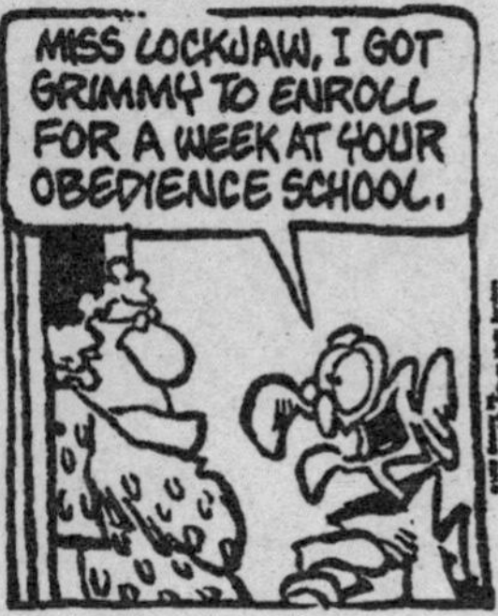
MISS LOCKJAW, I GOT GRIMMY TO ENROLL FOR A WEEK AT YOUR OBEDIENCE SCHOOL.

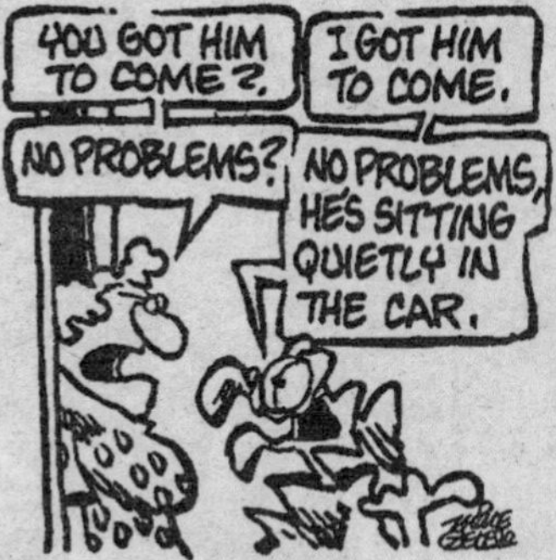
YOU GOT HIM TO COME?
I GOT HIM TO COME.
NO PROBLEMS?
NO PROBLEMS, HE'S SITTING QUIETLY IN THE CAR.

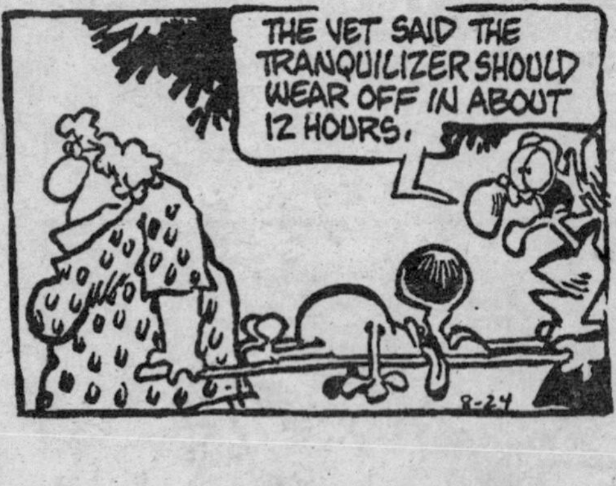
THE VET SAID THE TRANQUILIZER SHOULD WEAR OFF IN ABOUT 12 HOURS.
8-24

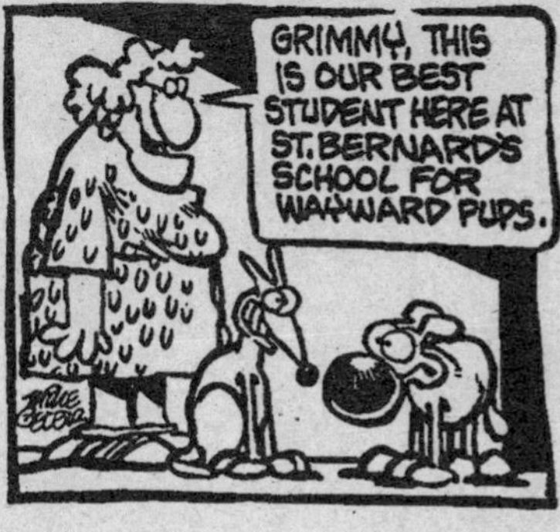
GRIMMY, THIS IS OUR BEST STUDENT HERE AT ST. BERNARD'S SCHOOL FOR WAYWARD PUPS.

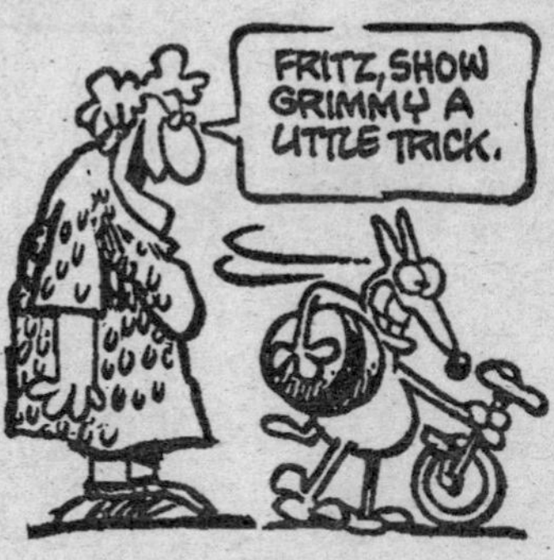
FRITZ, SHOW GRIMMY A LITTLE TRICK.

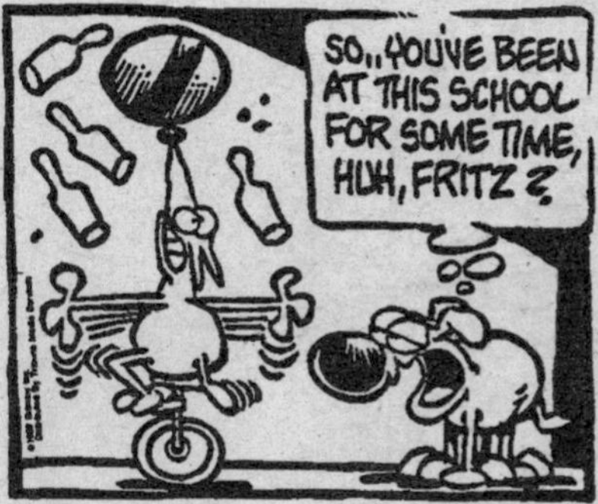
SO.. YOU'VE BEEN AT THIS SCHOOL FOR SOME TIME, HUH, FRITZ ?

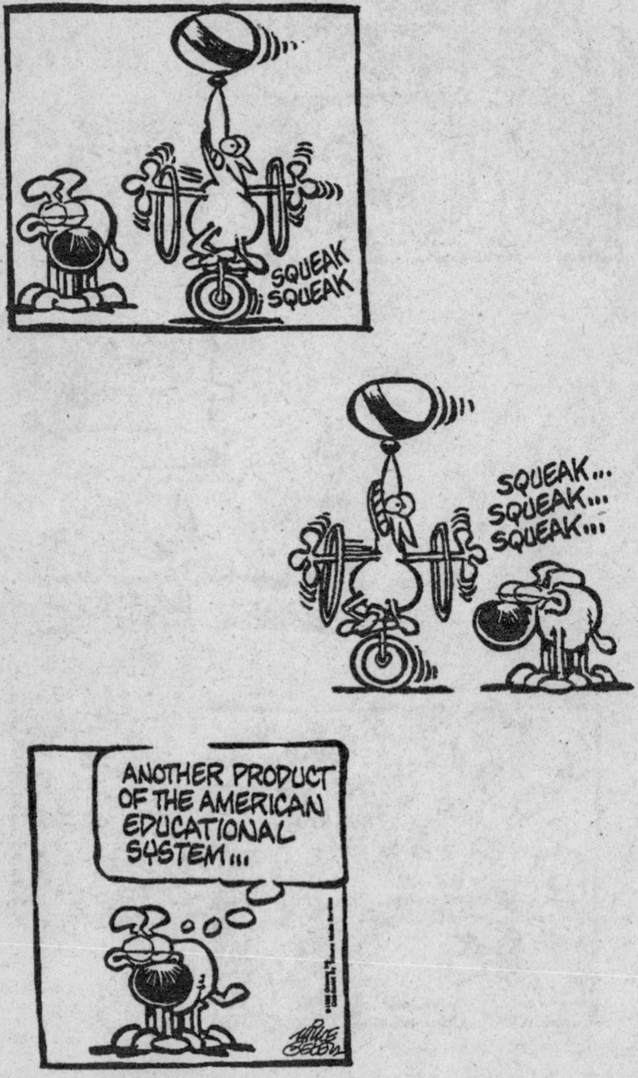
SQUEAK
SQUEAK
SQUEAK...
SQUEAK...
SQUEAK...
ANOTHER PRODUCT OF THE AMERICAN EDUCATIONAL SYSTEM...

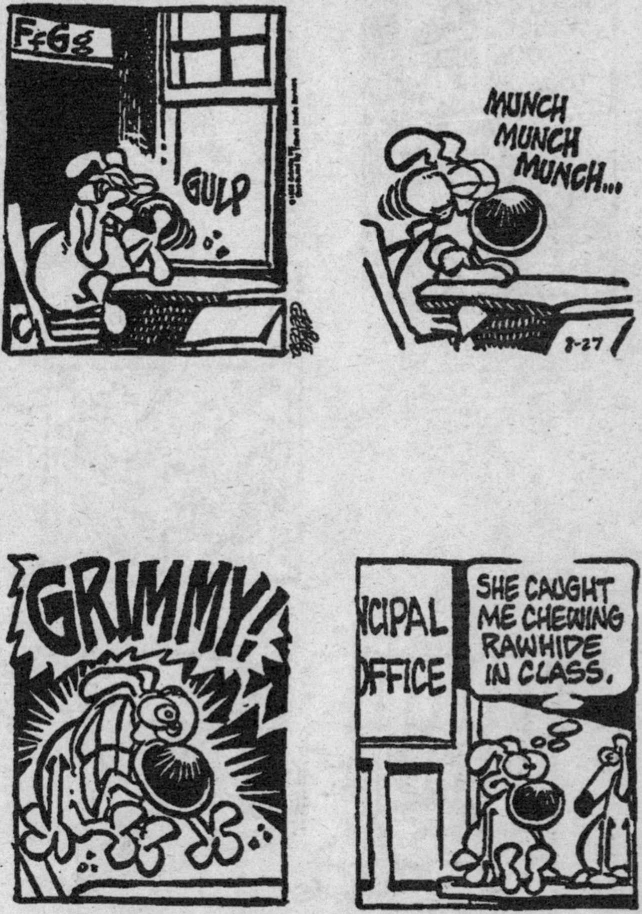
FfGg
GULP
MUNCH MUNCH MUNCH...
8-27
GRIMMY!
NCIPAL OFFICE
SHE CAUGHT ME CHEWING RAWHIDE IN CLASS.

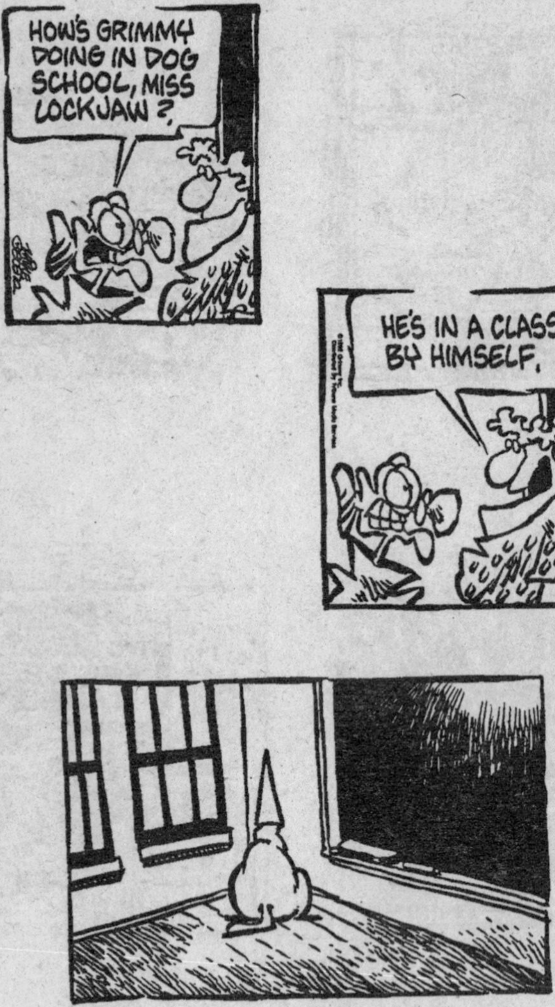
HOW'S GRIMMY DOING IN DOG SCHOOL, MISS LOCKJAW?
HE'S IN A CLASS BY HIMSELF.

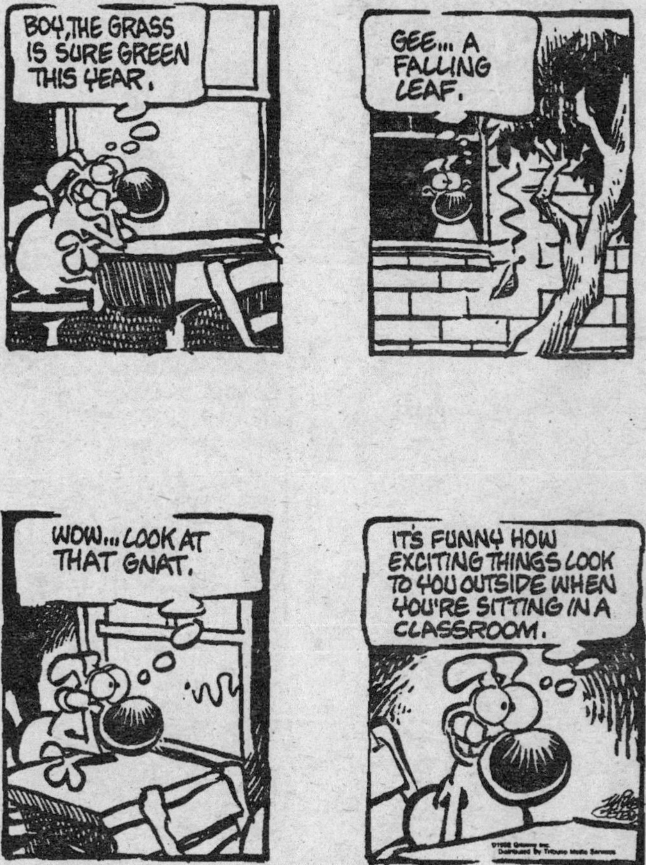
BOY, THE GRASS IS SURE GREEN THIS YEAR.
GEE... A FALLING LEAF.
WOW... LOOK AT THAT GNAT.
IT'S FUNNY HOW EXCITING THINGS LOOK TO YOU OUTSIDE WHEN YOU'RE SITTING IN A CLASSROOM.

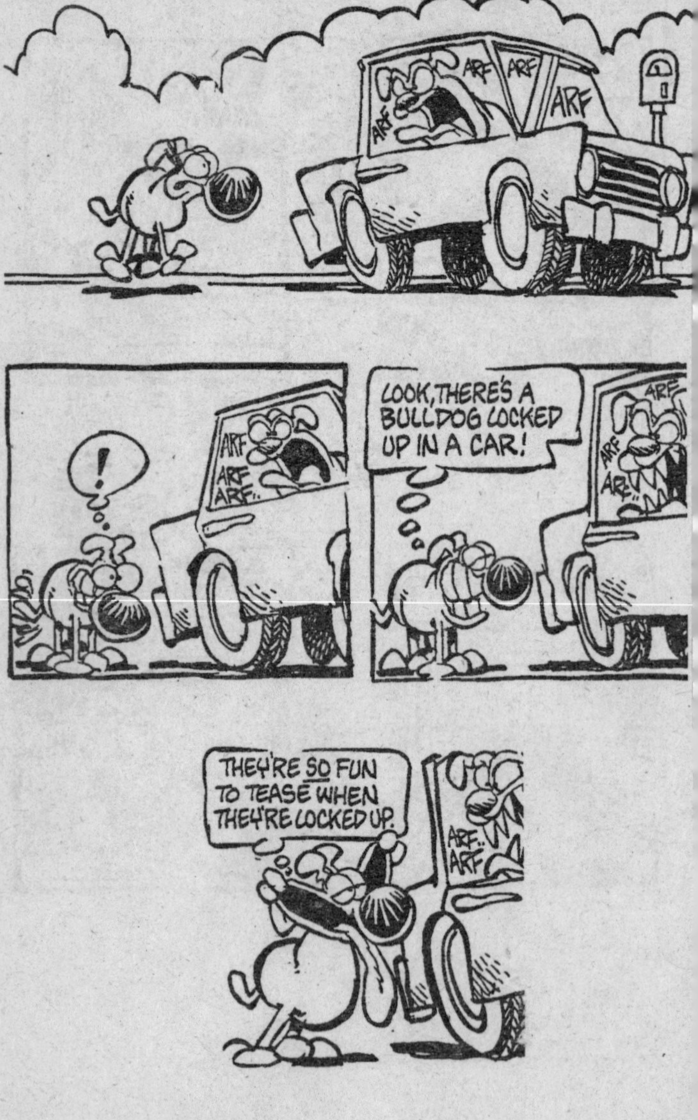
ARF
ARF
ARF
ARF
ARF
ARF
ARF..
!
LOOK, THERE'S A BULLDOG LOCKED UP IN A CAR!
ARF
ARF
ARF..
THEY'RE SO FUN TO TEASE WHEN THEY'RE LOCKED UP.
ARF..
ARF

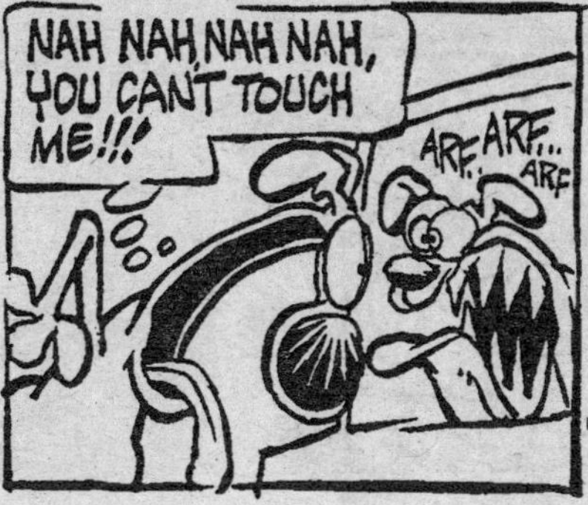
NAH NAH, NAH NAH, YOU CAN'T TOUCH ME!!!
ARF. ARF... ARF

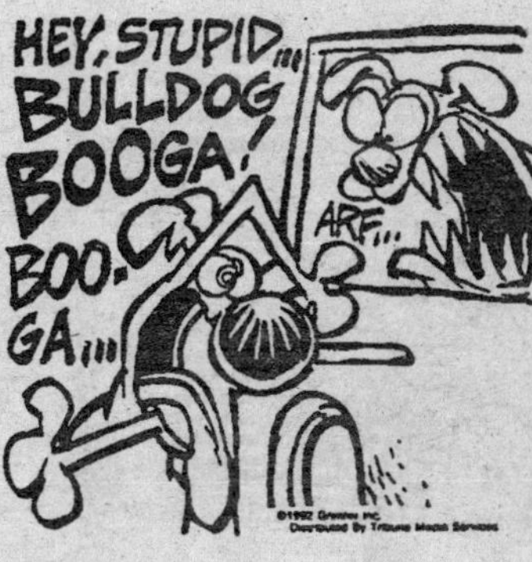
HEY, STUPID... BULLDOG BOOGA! BOO-GA...
ARF...

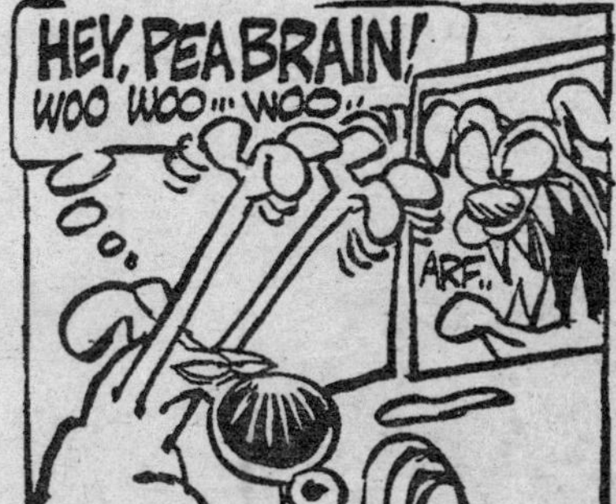
HEY, PEABRAIN! WOO WOO... WOO..
ARF..

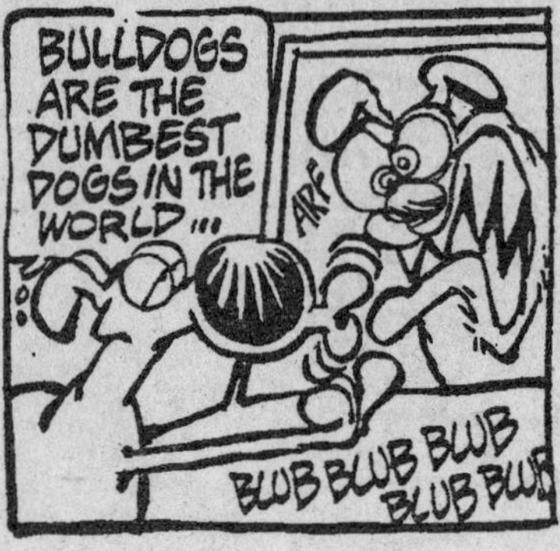
BULLDOGS ARE THE DUMBEST DOGS IN THE WORLD...
ARF
BLUB BLUB BLUB BLUB BLUB

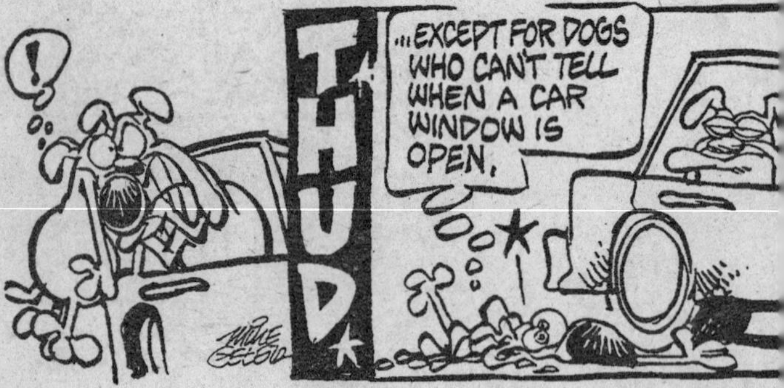
!
THUD
...EXCEPT FOR DOGS WHO CAN'T TELL WHEN A CAR WINDOW IS OPEN.

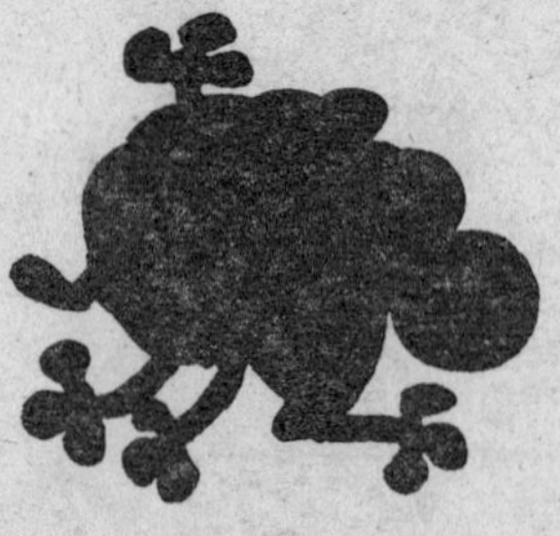

DEAR MZ. GOOSE, MY DOG NEVER COMES WHEN I CALL HIM...
3/11
WHAT DO YOU CALL TO GET GRIMMY TO COME?
911

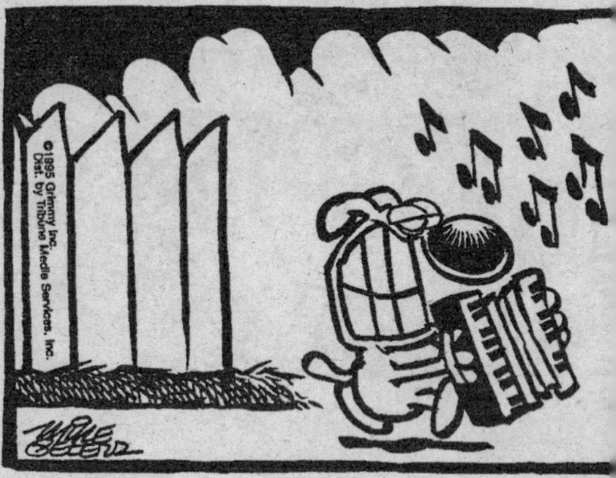
©1995 Grimmy Inc.
Dist. by Tribune Media Services, Inc.

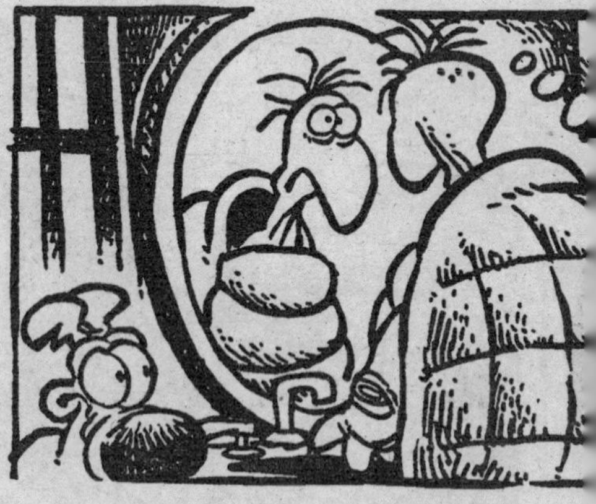

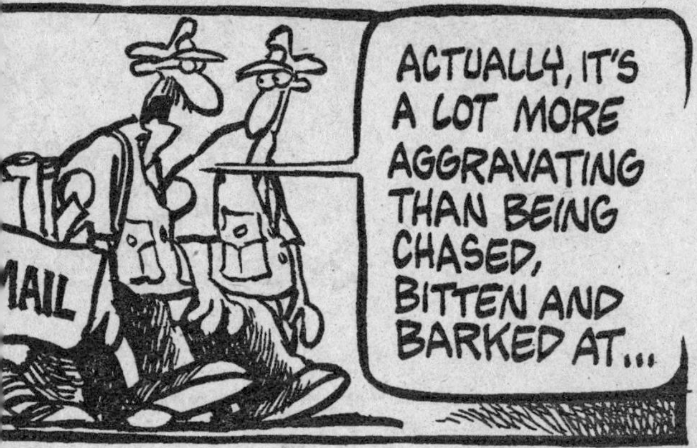
MAIL
ACTUALLY, IT'S A LOT MORE AGGRAVATING THAN BEING CHASED, BITTEN AND BARKED AT...

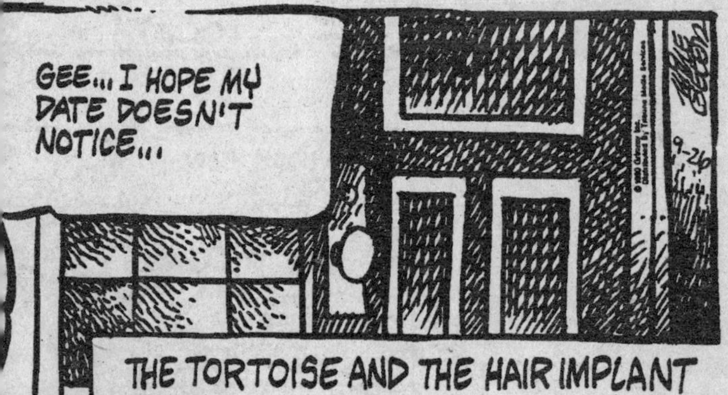
GEE... I HOPE MY DATE DOESN'T NOTICE...
9-26

THE TORTOISE AND THE HAIR IMPLANT

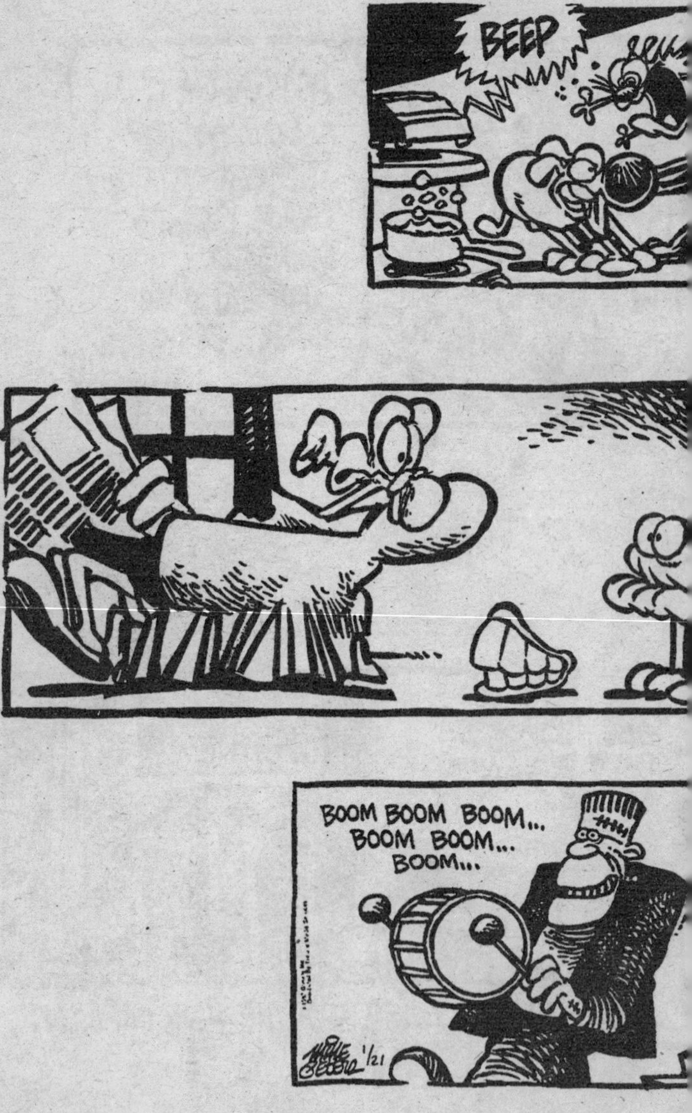
BEEP
BOOM BOOM BOOM...
BOOM BOOM...
BOOM...
1/21

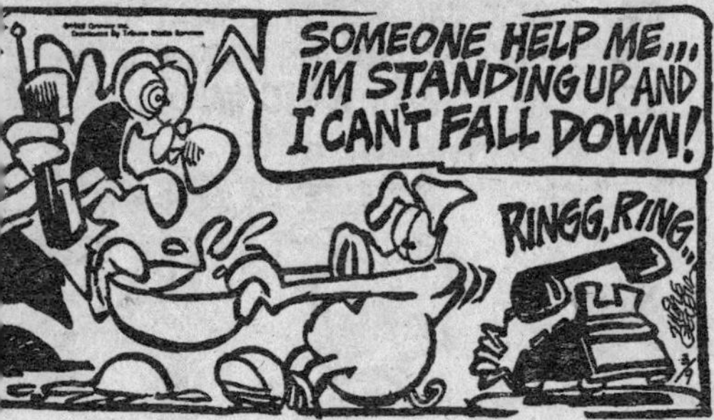
SOMEONE HELP ME... I'M STANDING UP AND I CAN'T FALL DOWN!
RINGG, RING...

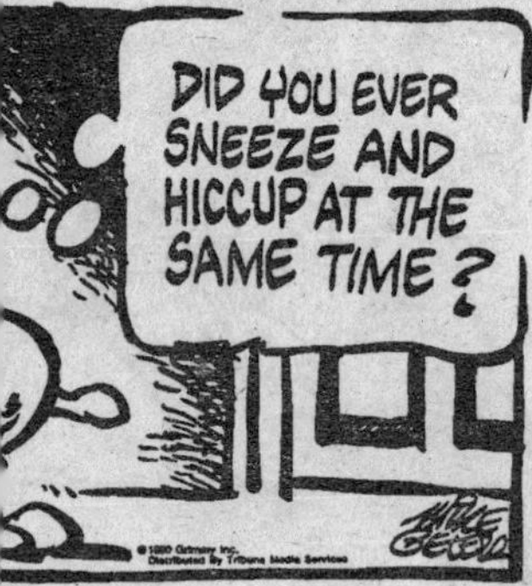
DID YOU EVER SNEEZE AND HICCUP AT THE SAME TIME?

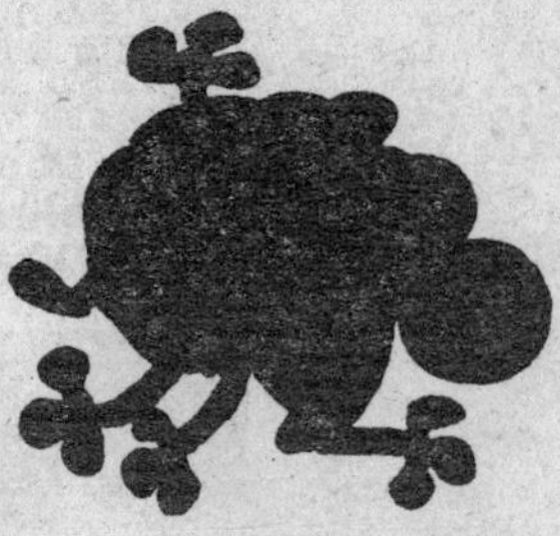

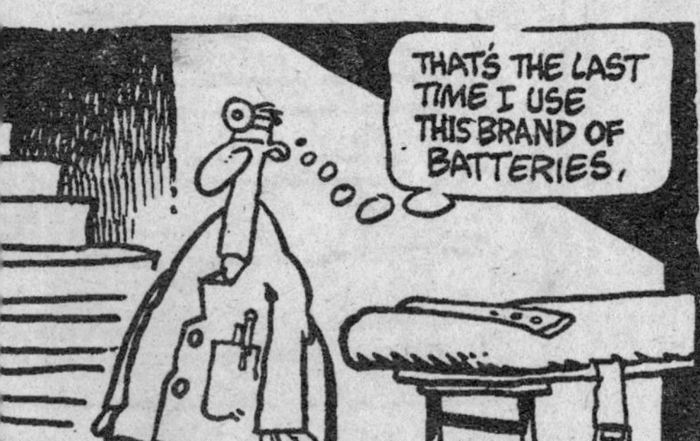
THAT'S THE LAST TIME I USE THIS BRAND OF BATTERIES.

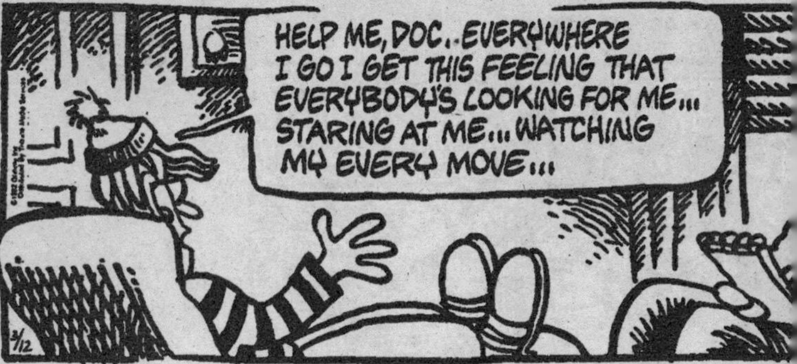
HELP ME, DOC..EVERYWHERE I GO I GET THIS FEELING THAT EVERYBODY'S LOOKING FOR ME... STARING AT ME... WATCHING MY EVERY MOVE...
3/12

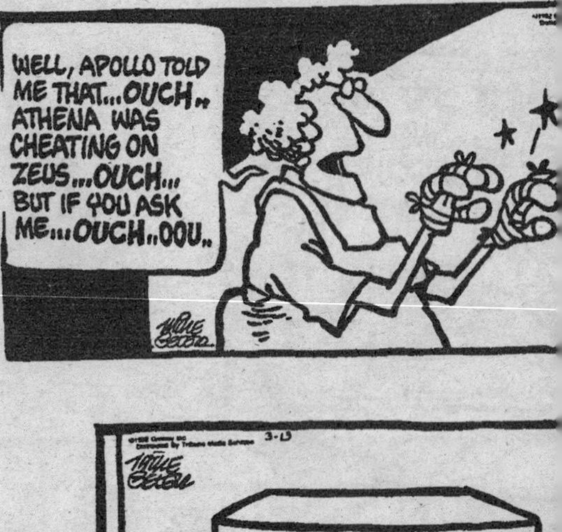
WELL, APOLLO TOLD ME THAT...OUCH.. ATHENA WAS CHEATING ON ZEUS...OUCH... BUT IF YOU ASK ME...OUCH..OOU..

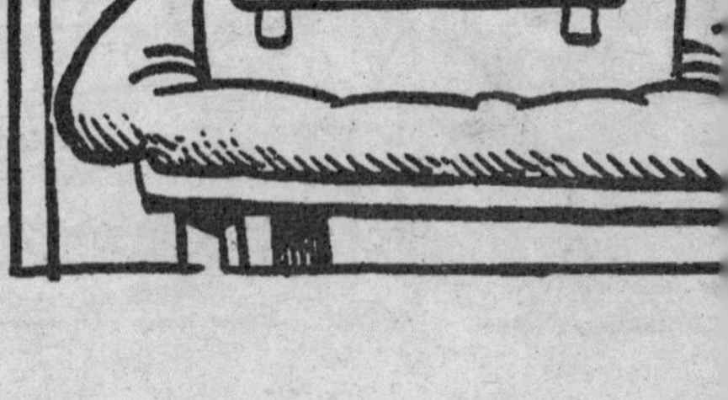
3-13

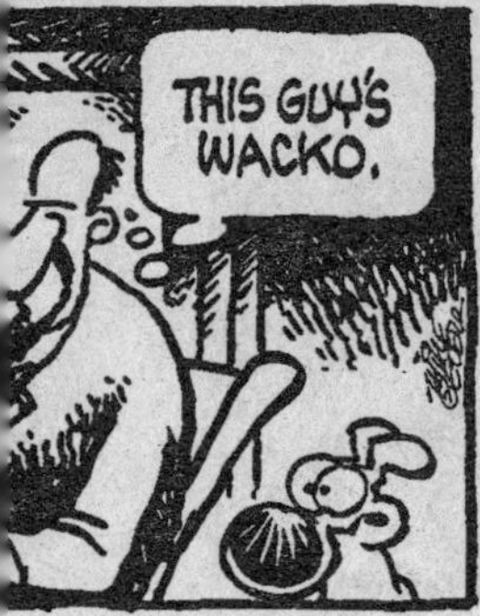
THIS GUY'S WACKO.

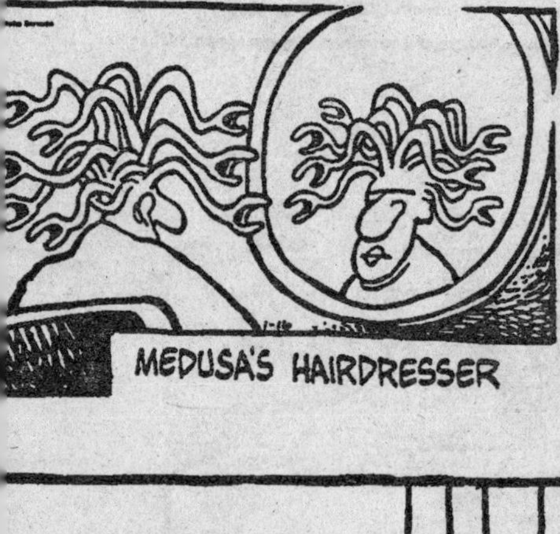

MEDUSA'S HAIRDRESSER

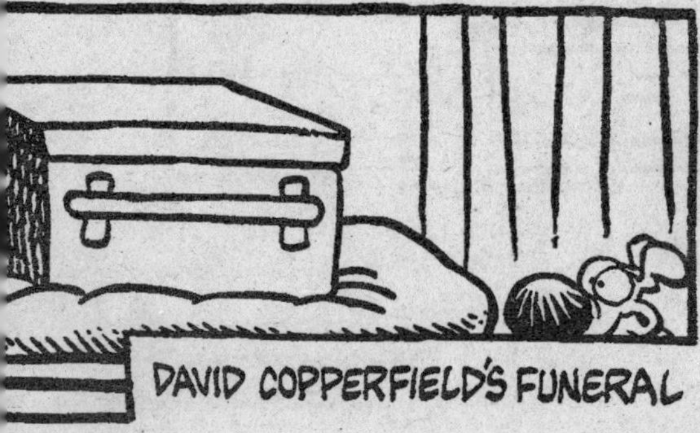

DAVID COPPERFIELD'S FUNERAL

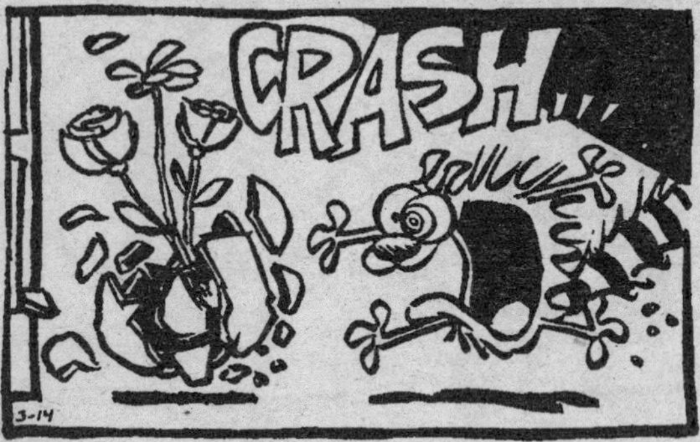
CRASH...
3-14

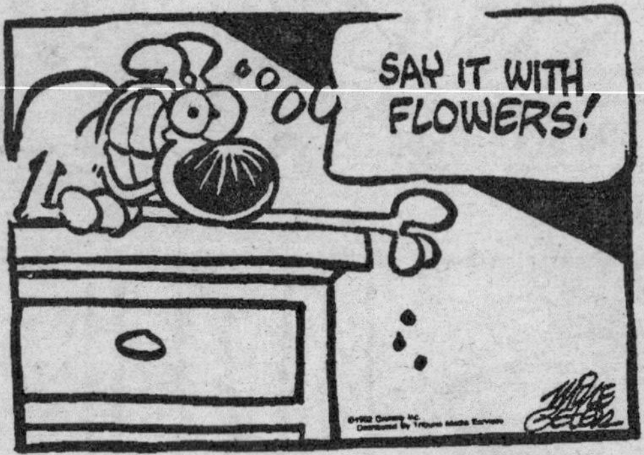
SAY IT WITH FLOWERS!

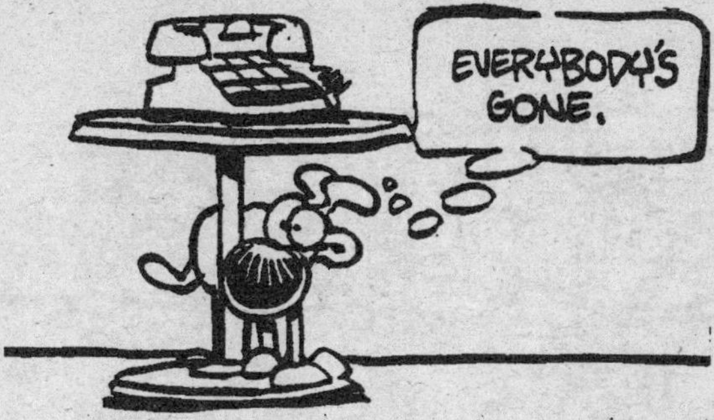
EVERYBODY'S GONE.

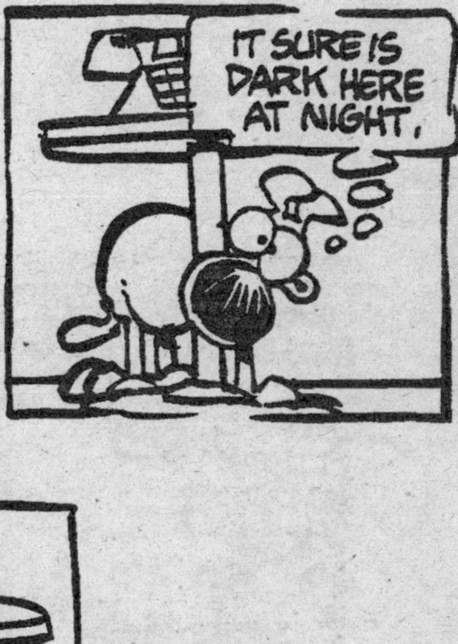
IT SURE IS DARK HERE AT NIGHT.

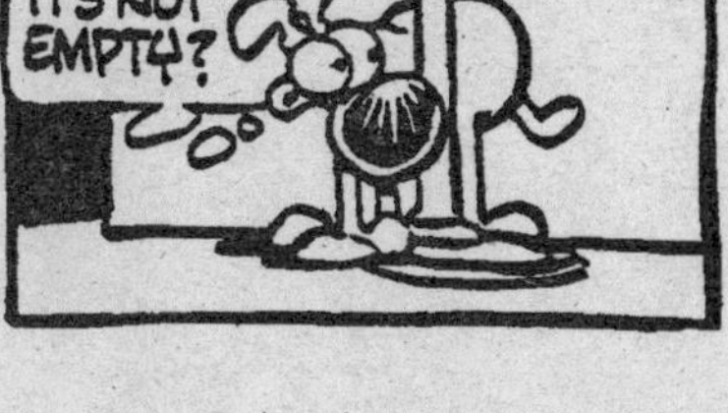
I HATE GUARDING AN EMPTY HOUSE, BUT WHAT IF IT'S NOT EMPTY?

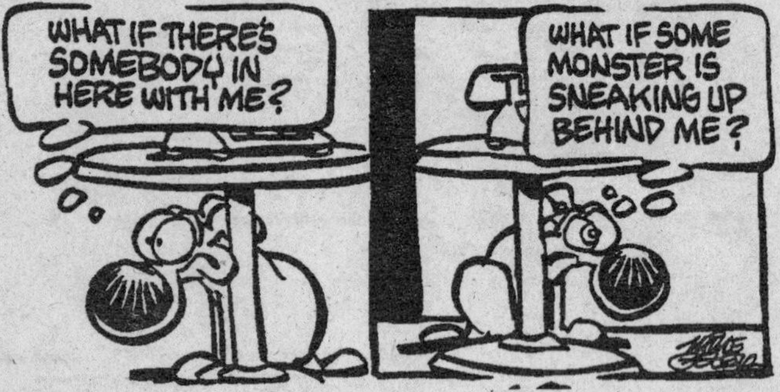
WHAT IF THERE'S SOMEBODY IN HERE WITH ME?
WHAT IF SOME MONSTER IS SNEAKING UP BEHIND ME?

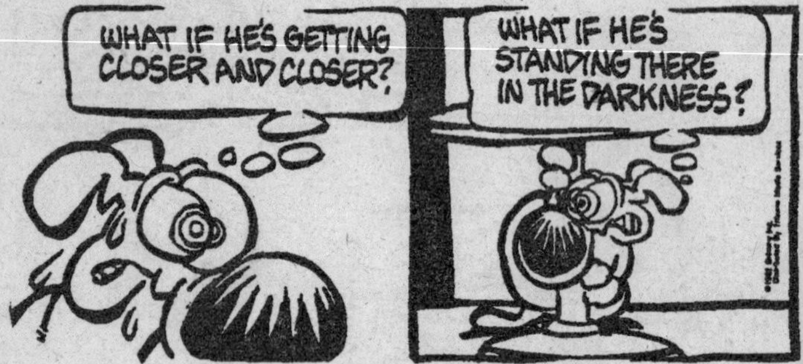
WHAT IF HE'S GETTING CLOSER AND CLOSER?
WHAT IF HE'S STANDING THERE IN THE DARKNESS?

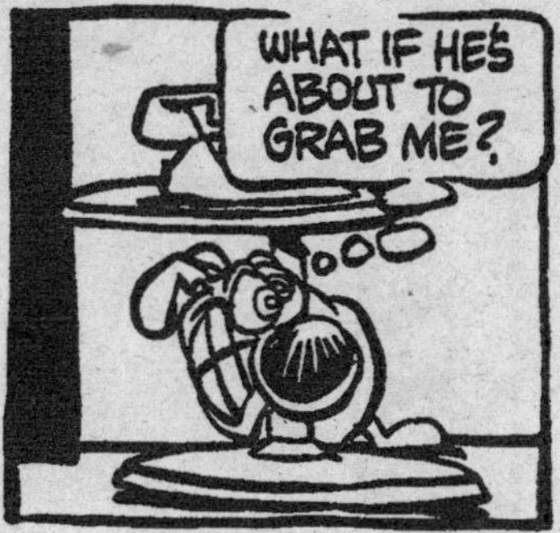
WHAT IF HE'S ABOUT TO GRAB ME?

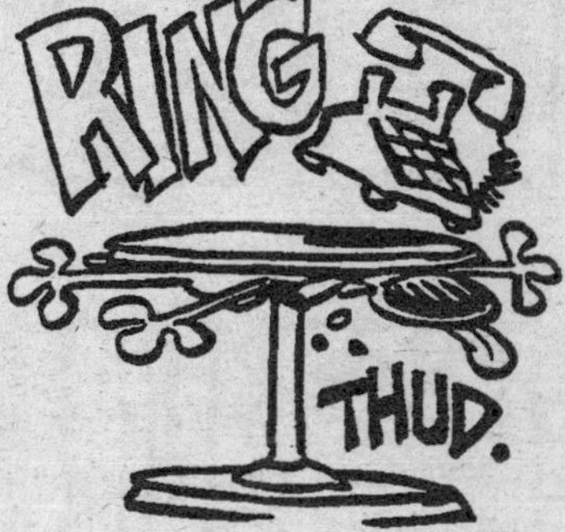
RING
THUD.

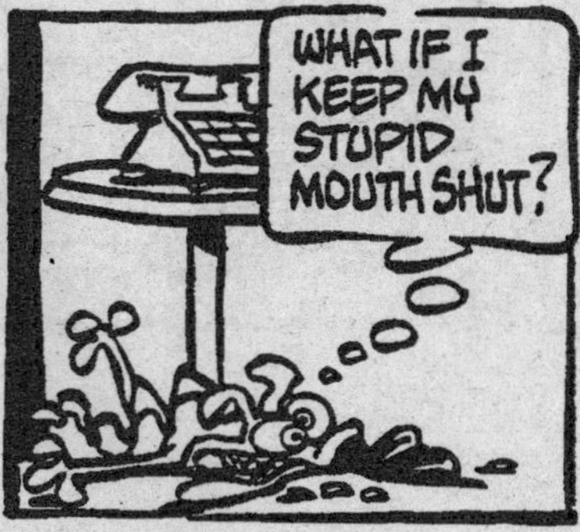
WHAT IF I KEEP MY STUPID MOUTH SHUT?

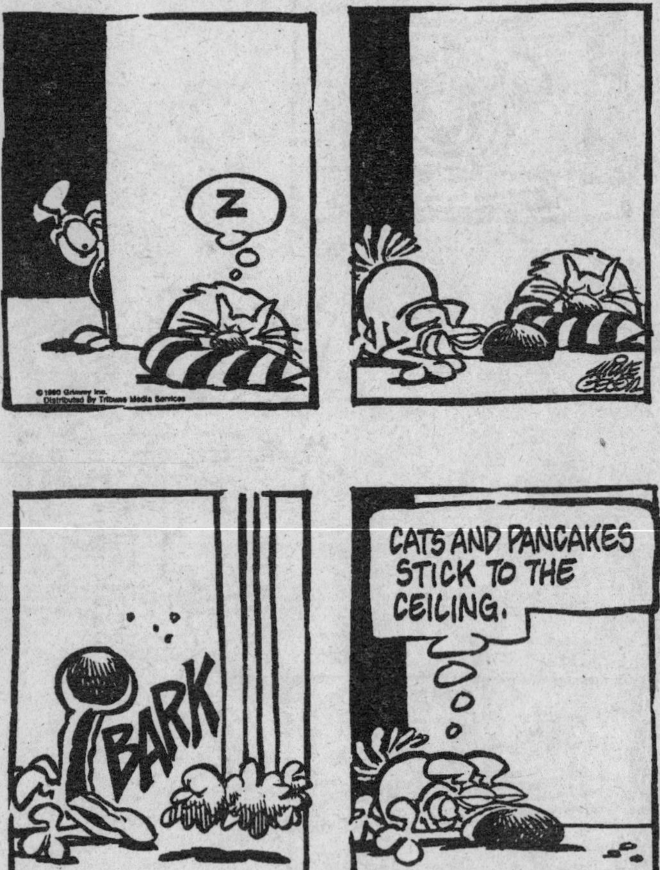
Z
BARK
CATS AND PANCAKES STICK TO THE CEILING.
© 1990 Grimmy Inc.
Distributed By Tribune Media Services

FAMOUS BOXERS IN HISTORY

3-17

JACK DEMPSEY

JOE LOUIS

SIZE 34 ONCE WORN BY WARREN BEATTY

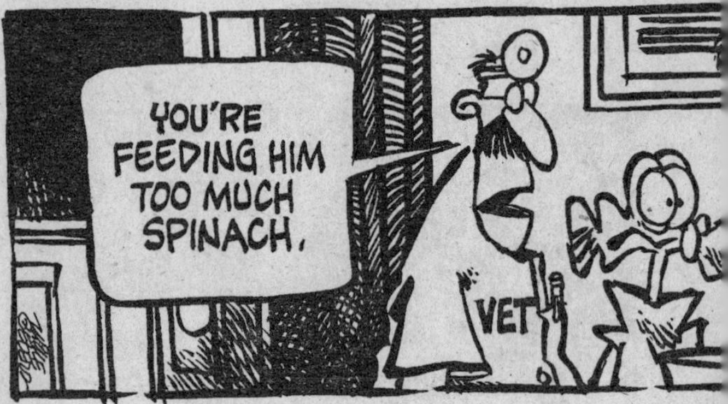
YOU'RE FEEDING HIM TOO MUCH SPINACH.
VET

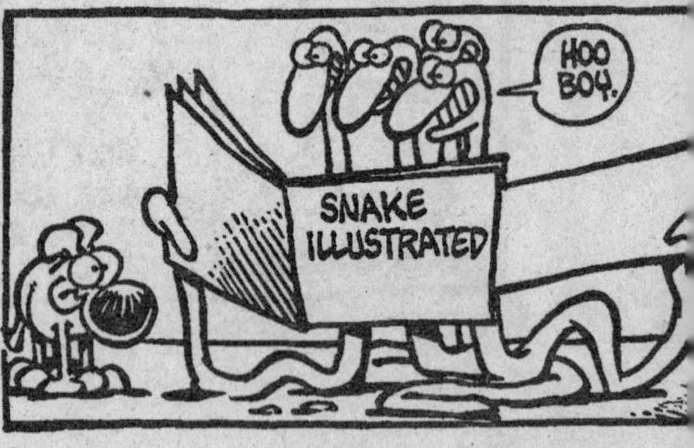
HOO BOY.
SNAKE ILLUSTRATED

THE SKIN-SHED ISSUE

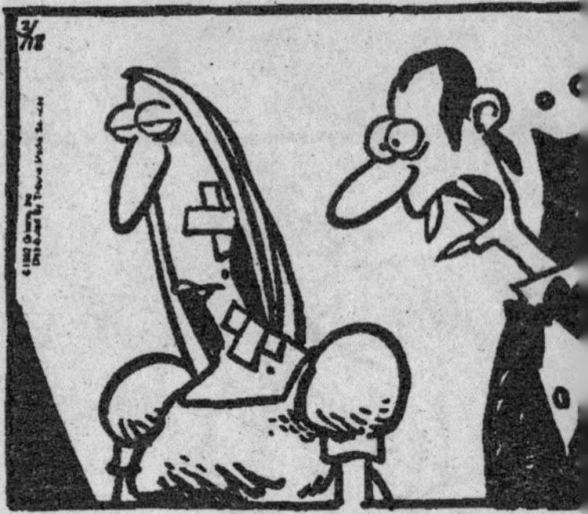

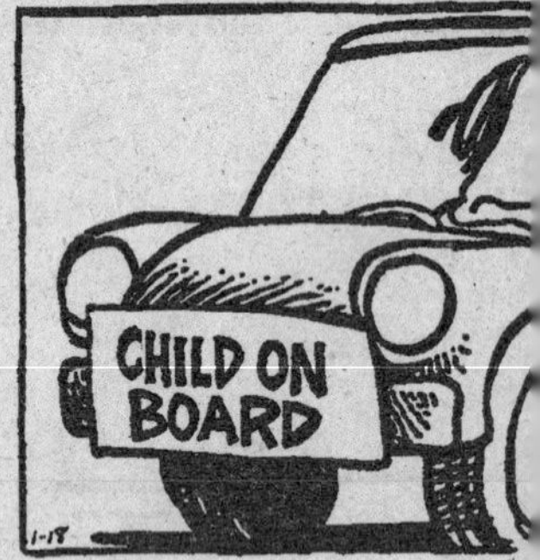
CHILD ON
BOARD
1-18

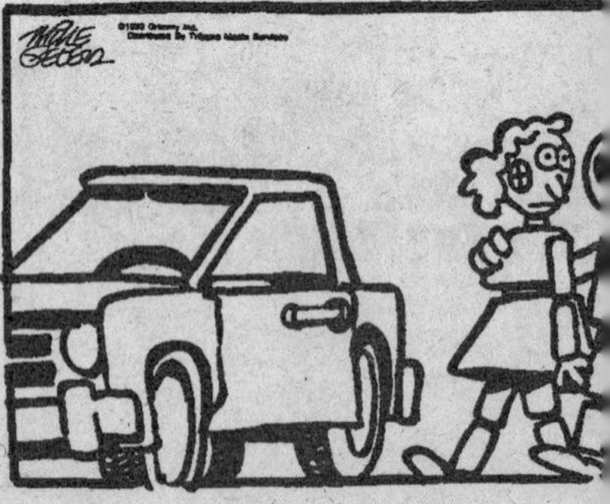

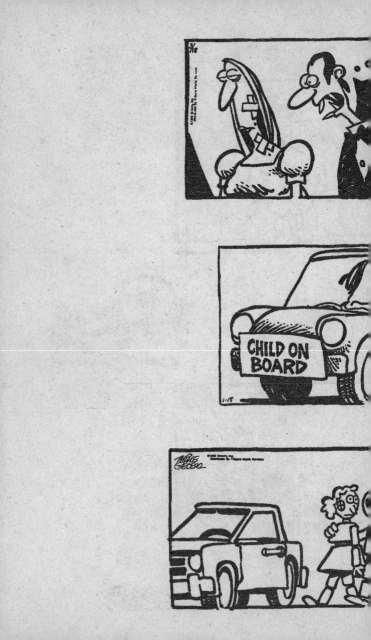

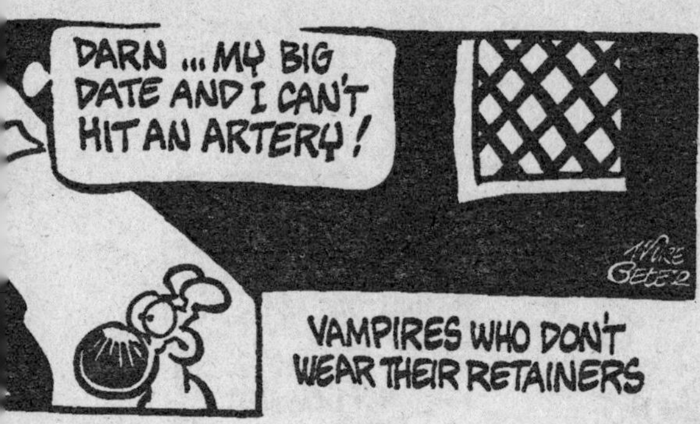
DARN ... MY BIG DATE AND I CAN'T HIT AN ARTERY!

VAMPIRES WHO DON'T WEAR THEIR RETAINERS

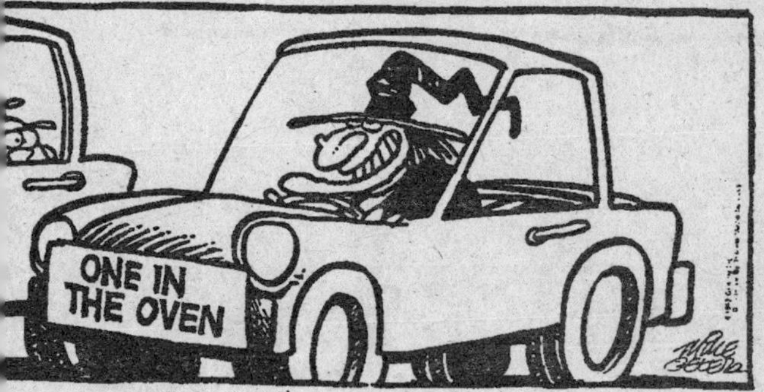
ONE IN THE OVEN

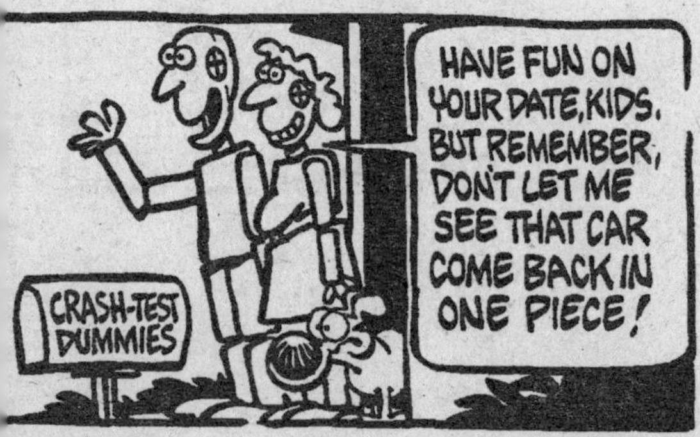
HAVE FUN ON YOUR DATE, KIDS. BUT REMEMBER, DON'T LET ME SEE THAT CAR COME BACK IN ONE PIECE!
CRASH-TEST DUMMIES

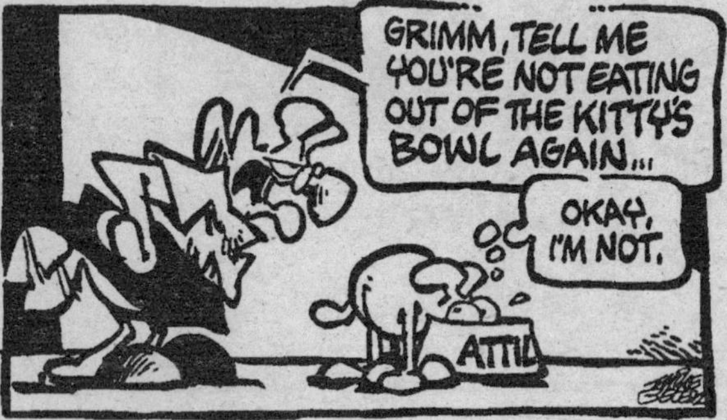
GRIMM, TELL ME YOU'RE NOT EATING OUT OF THE KITTY'S BOWL AGAIN...
OKAY, I'M NOT.
ATTIL

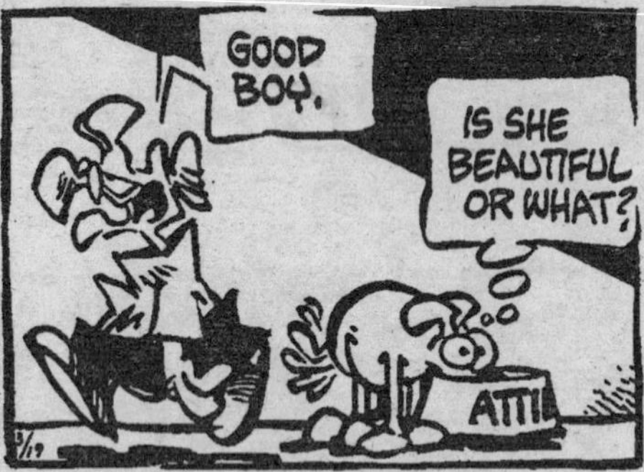
GOOD BOY.
IS SHE BEAUTIFUL OR WHAT?
ATTI
3/19

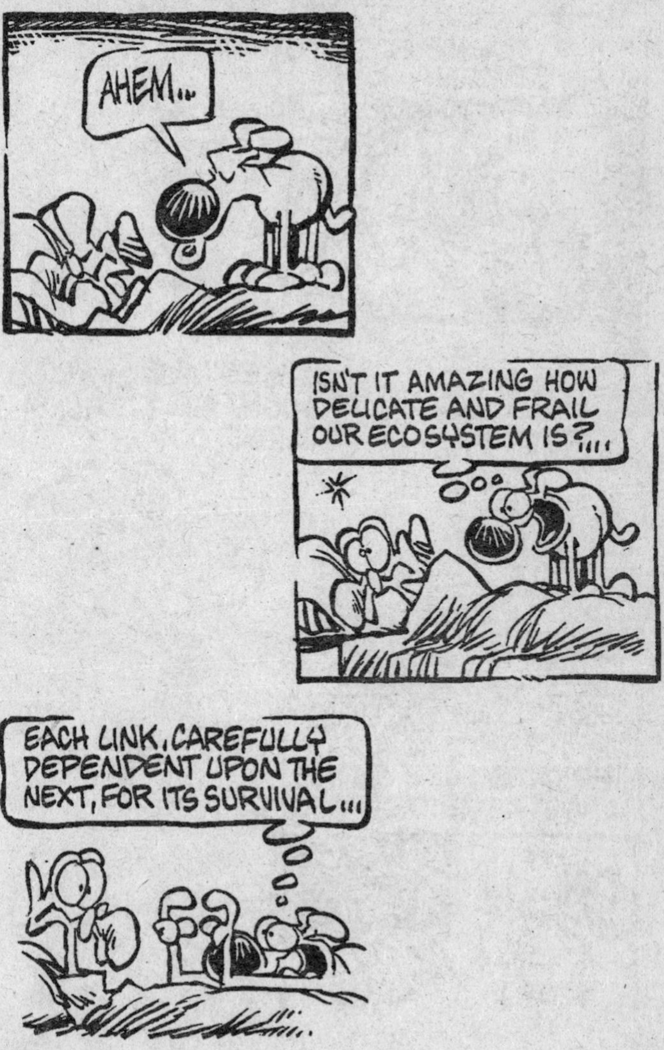
AHEM...
ISN'T IT AMAZING HOW DELICATE AND FRAIL OUR ECOSYSTEM IS?...
EACH LINK, CAREFULLY DEPENDENT UPON THE NEXT, FOR ITS SURVIVAL...

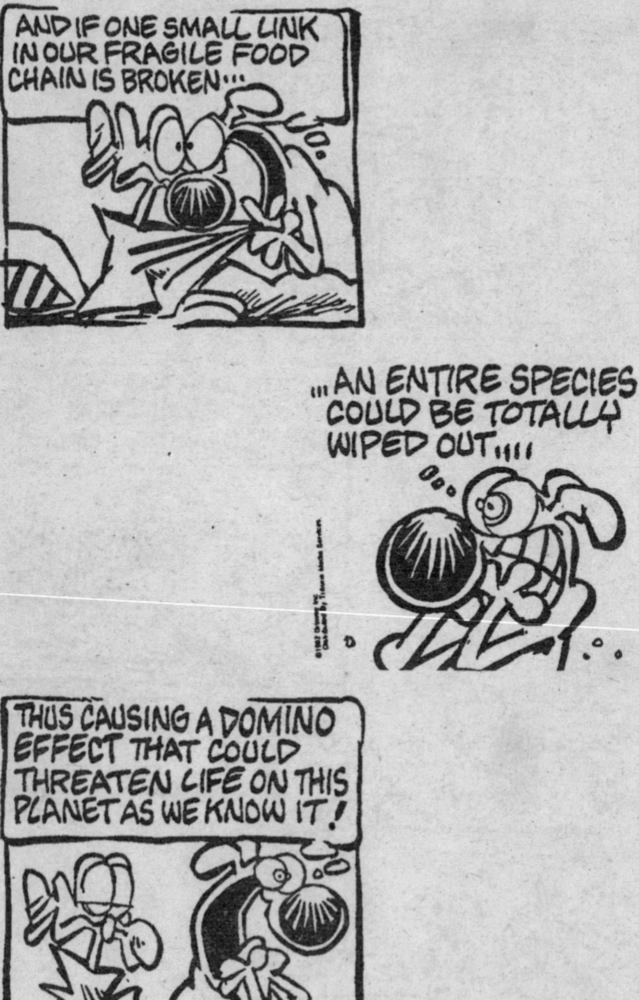
AND IF ONE SMALL LINK IN OUR FRAGILE FOOD CHAIN IS BROKEN...
...AN ENTIRE SPECIES COULD BE TOTALLY WIPED OUT....
THUS CAUSING A DOMINO EFFECT THAT COULD THREATEN LIFE ON THIS PLANET AS WE KNOW IT!

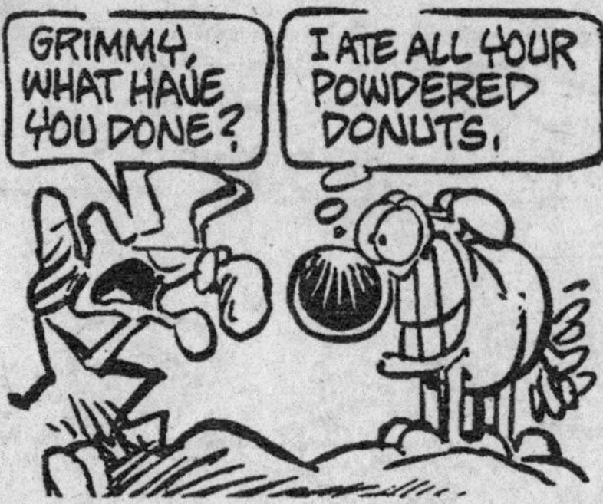
GRIMMY, WHAT HAVE YOU DONE?
I ATE ALL YOUR POWDERED DONUTS.

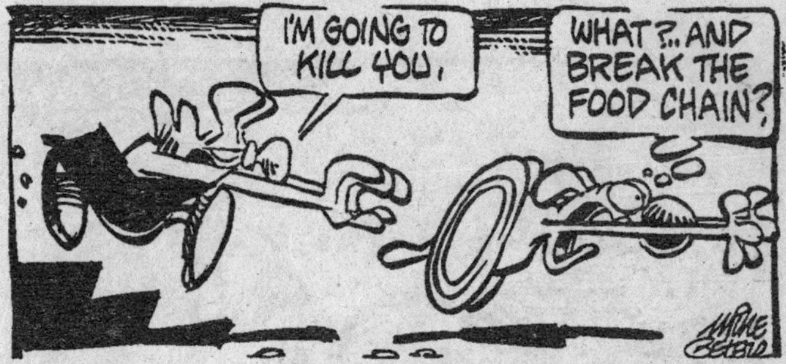
I'M GOING TO KILL YOU.
WHAT?.. AND BREAK THE FOOD CHAIN?
MIKE PETERS

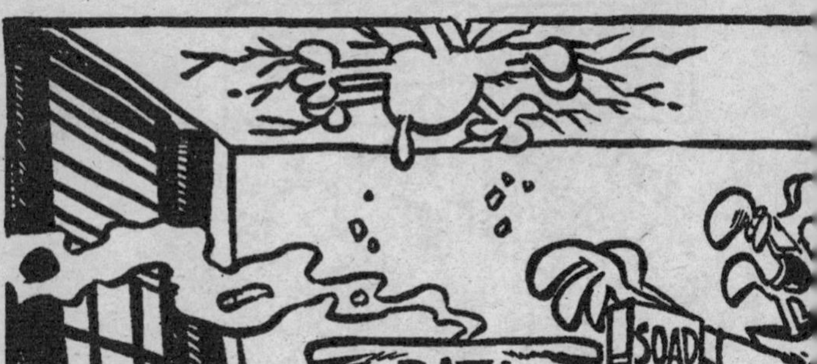
BATH
SOAP

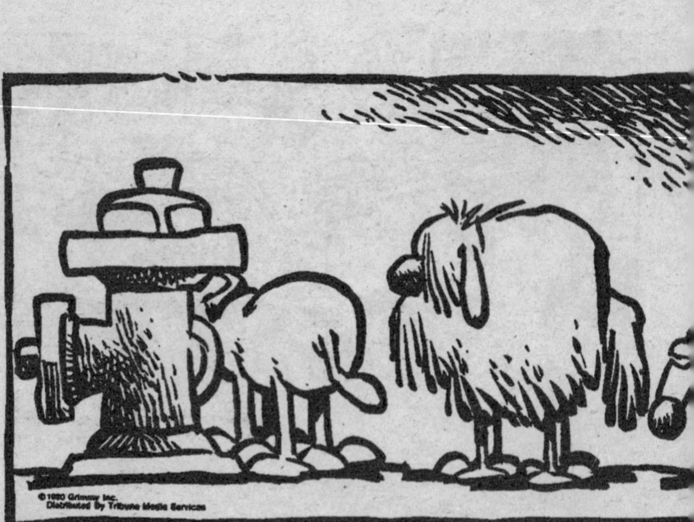
© 1990 Grimmy Inc.
Distributed By Tribune Media Services

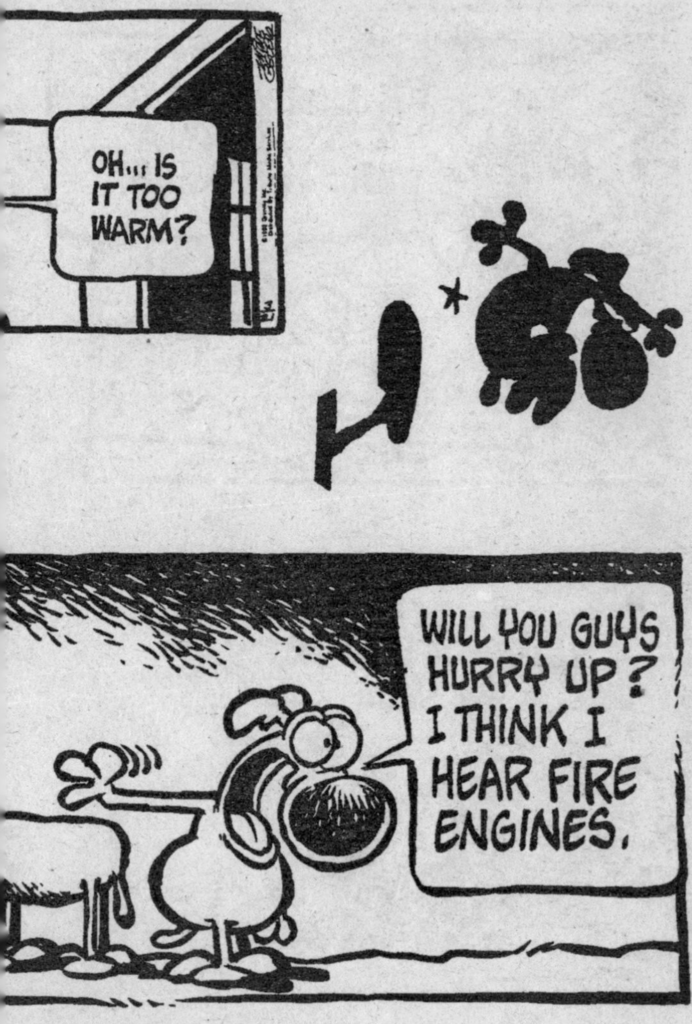
OH... IS IT TOO WARM?
WILL YOU GUYS HURRY UP? I THINK I HEAR FIRE ENGINES.

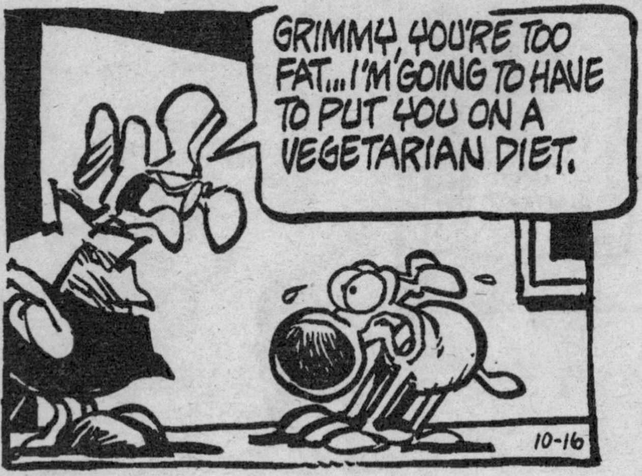
GRIMMY, YOU'RE TOO FAT... I'M GOING TO HAVE TO PUT YOU ON A VEGETARIAN DIET.
10-16

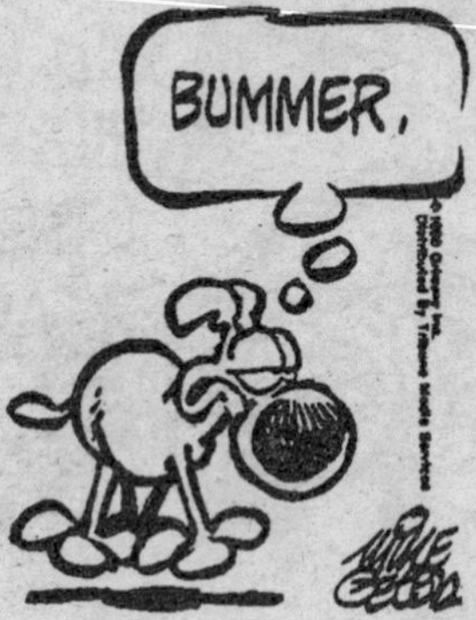
BUMMER.
Distributed by Tribune Media Services

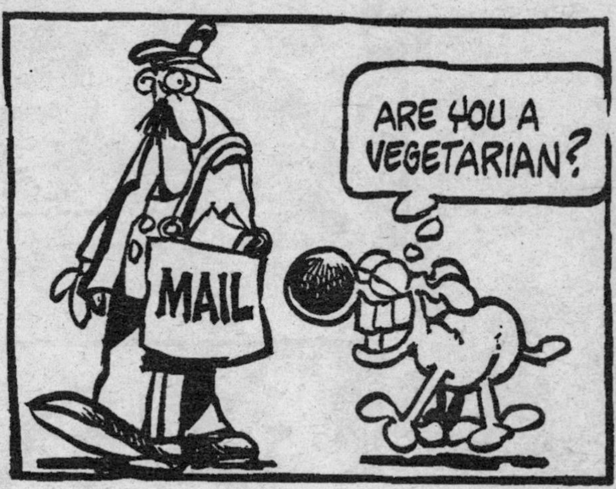
ARE YOU A VEGETARIAN?
MAIL

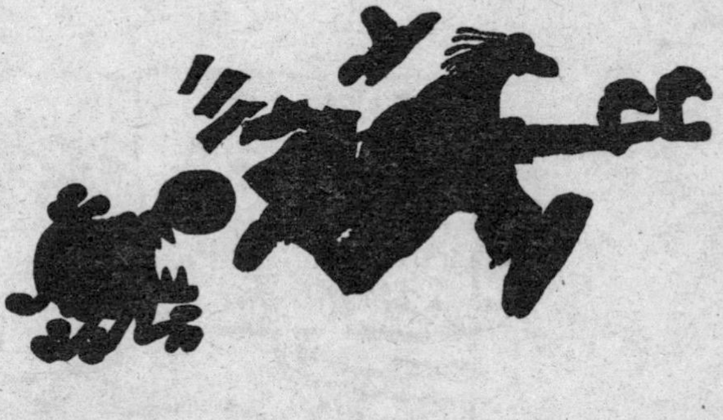

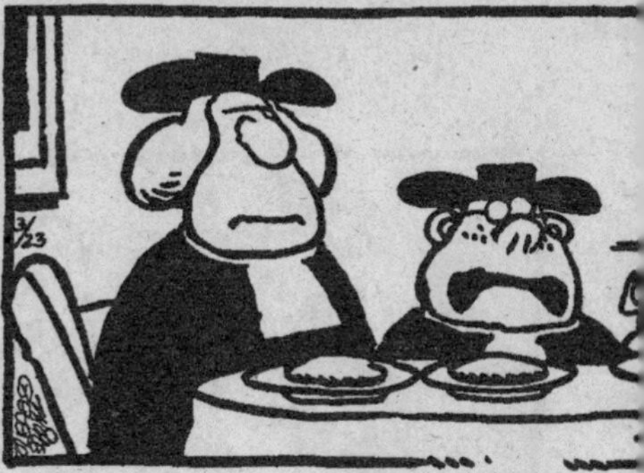
3/23

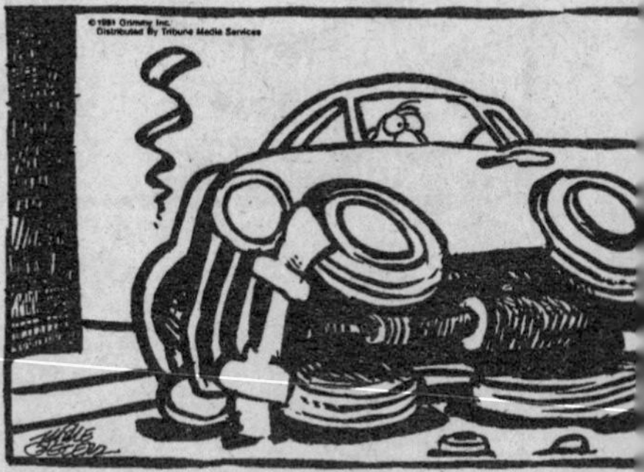
© 1991 Grimmy Inc.
Distributed By Tribune Media Services

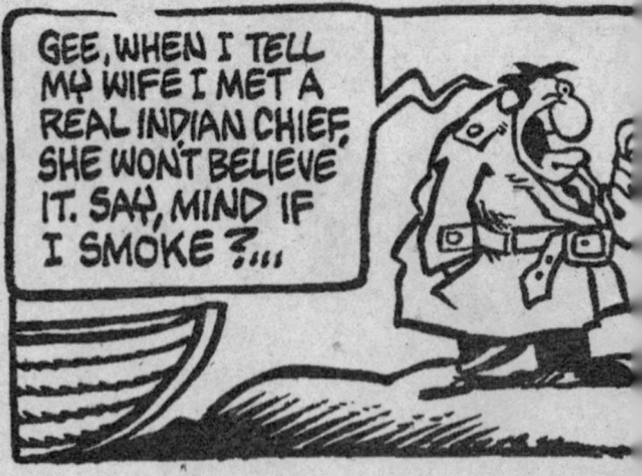
GEE, WHEN I TELL MY WIFE I MET A REAL INDIAN CHIEF, SHE WON'T BELIEVE IT. SAY, MIND IF I SMOKE?...

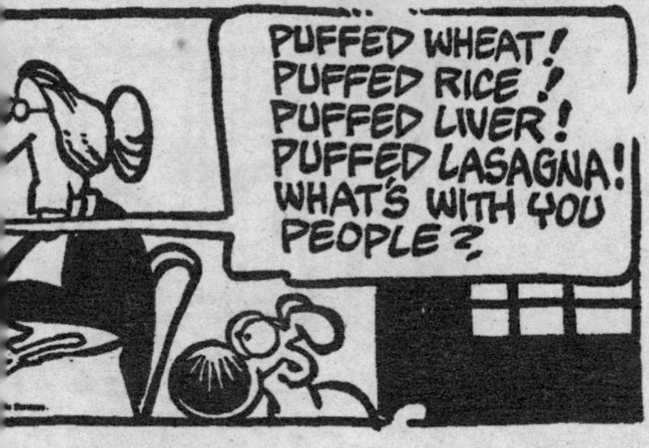
PUFFED WHEAT! PUFFED RICE! PUFFED LIVER! PUFFED LASAGNA! WHAT'S WITH YOU PEOPLE?

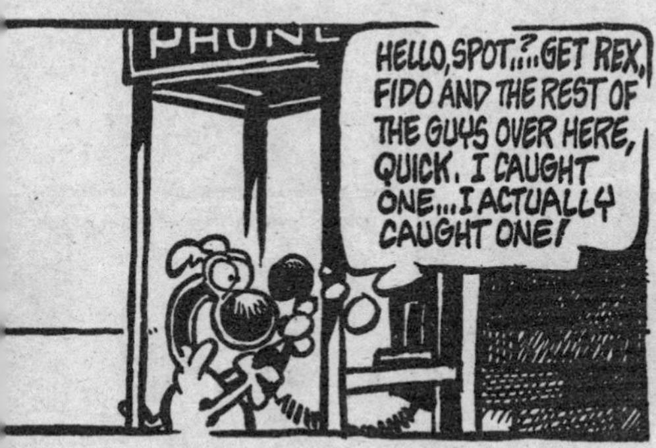
PHONE
HELLO, SPOT...?...GET REX, FIDO AND THE REST OF THE GUYS OVER HERE, QUICK. I CAUGHT ONE...I ACTUALLY CAUGHT ONE!

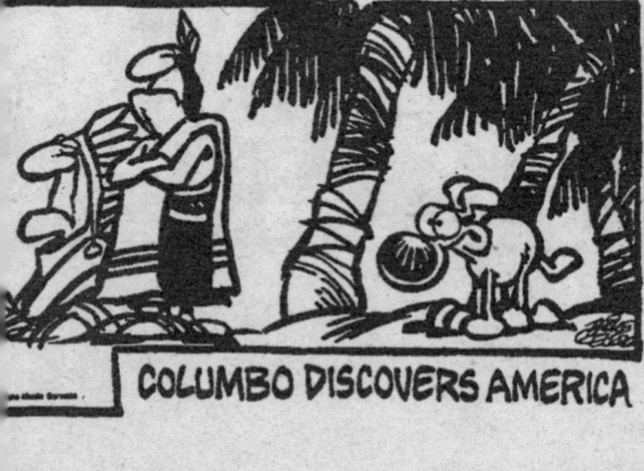
COLUMBO DISCOVERS AMERICA

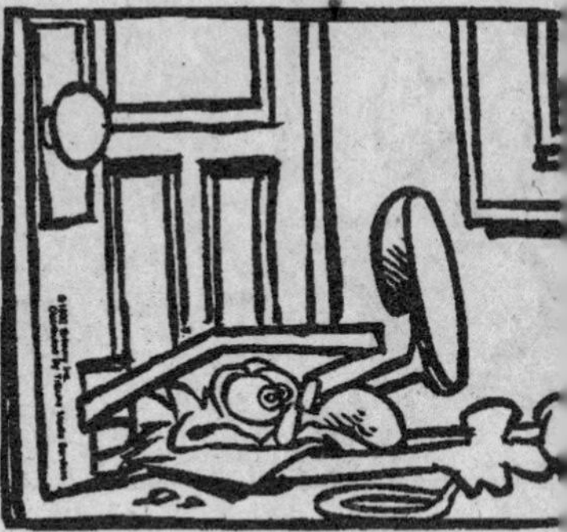

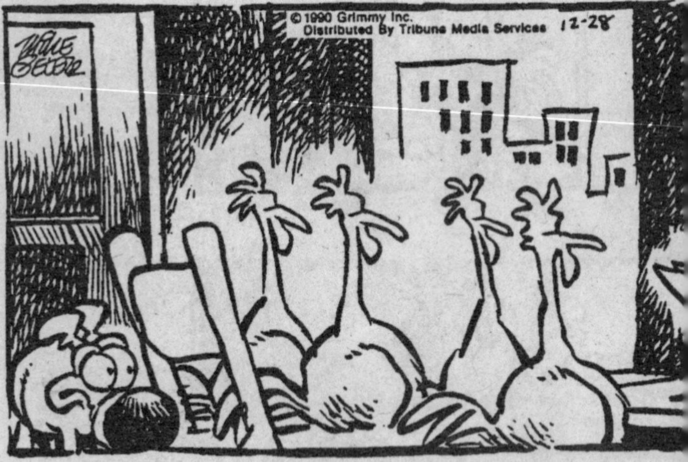
© 1990 Grimmy Inc.
Distributed By Tribune Media Services 12-28

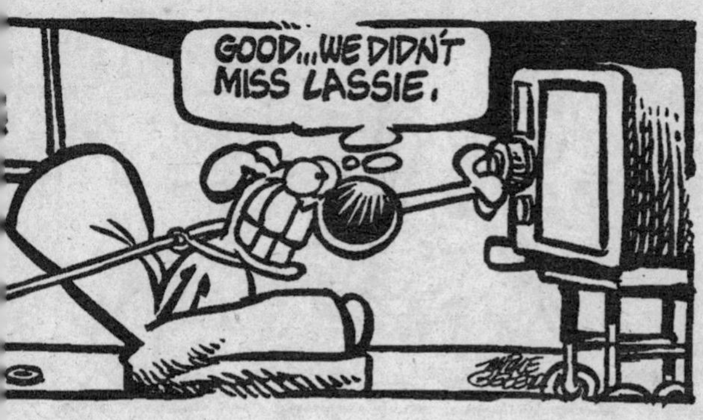
GOOD...WE DIDN'T MISS LASSIE.

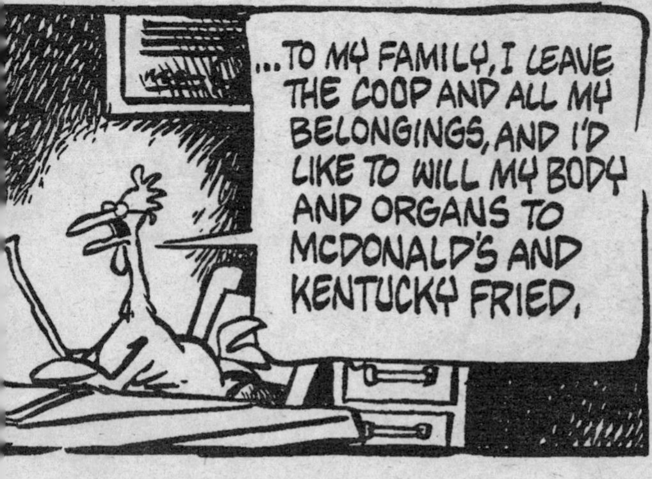
...TO MY FAMILY, I LEAVE THE COOP AND ALL MY BELONGINGS, AND I'D LIKE TO WILL MY BODY AND ORGANS TO MCDONALD'S AND KENTUCKY FRIED.

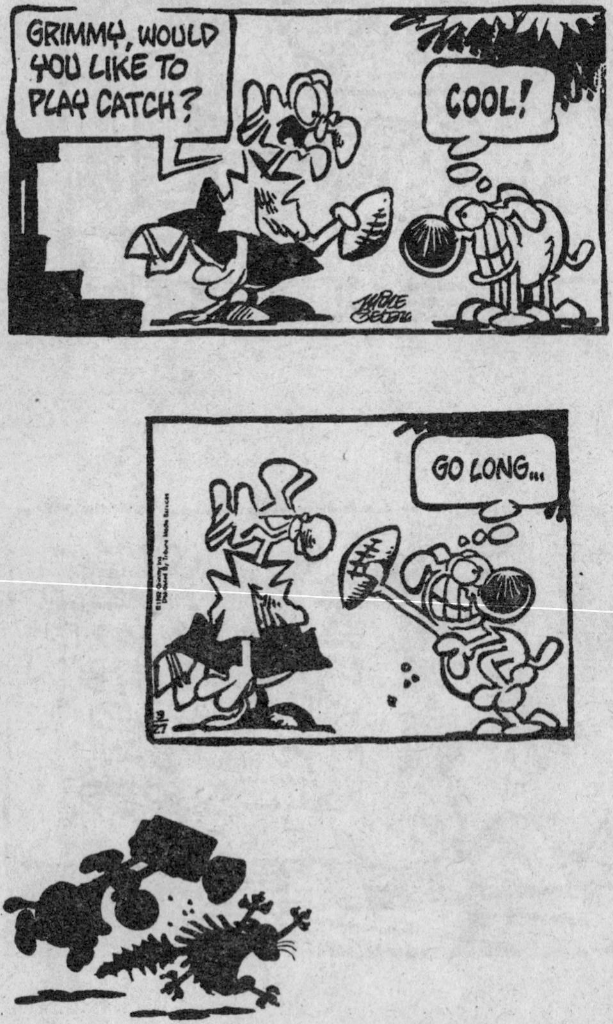
GRIMMY, WOULD YOU LIKE TO PLAY CATCH?
COOL!
GO LONG...

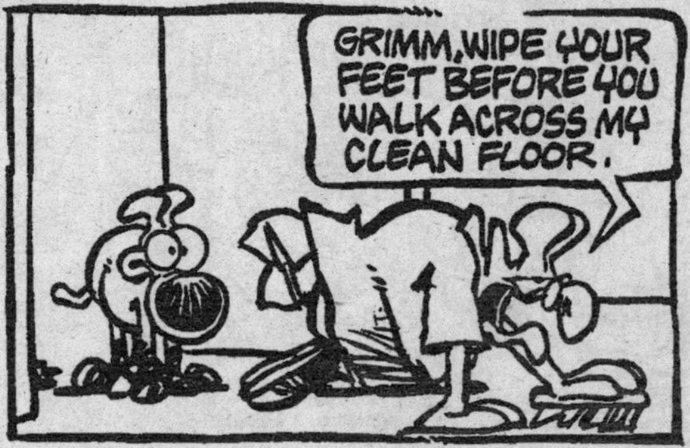
GRIMM, WIPE YOUR FEET BEFORE YOU WALK ACROSS MY CLEAN FLOOR.

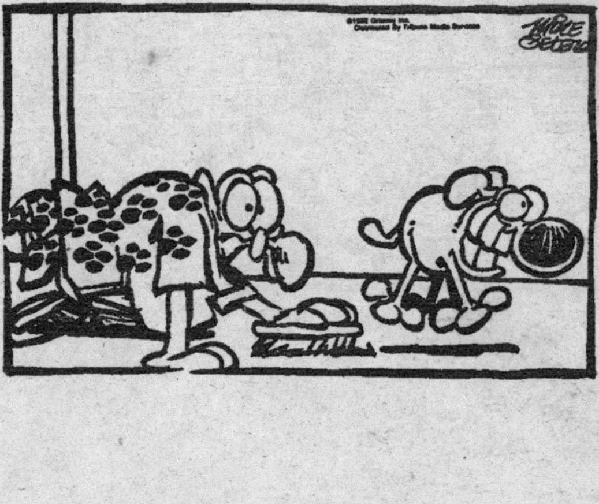

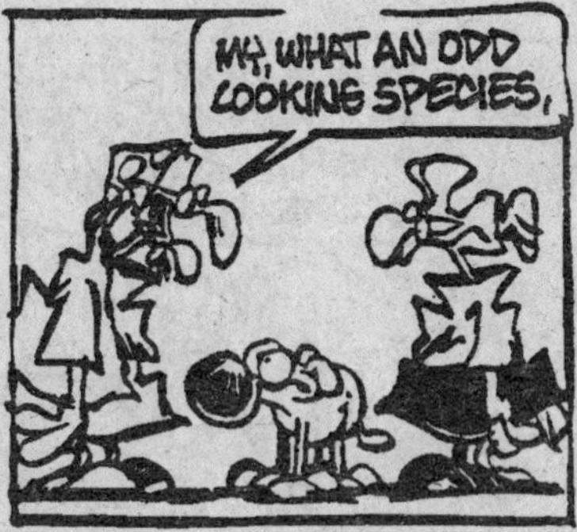
MY, WHAT AN ODD LOOKING SPECIES.

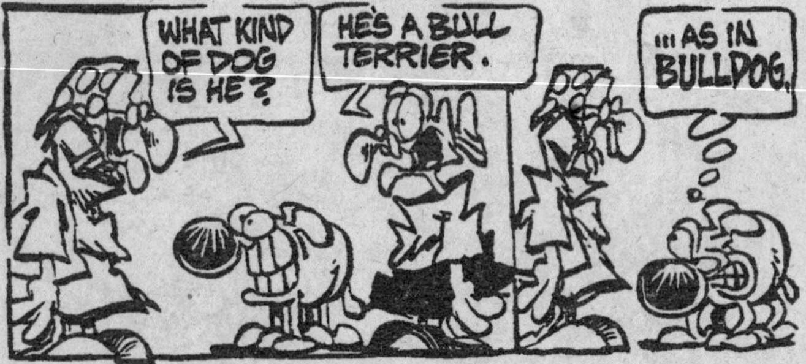
WHAT KIND OF DOG IS HE?
HE'S A BULL TERRIER.
...AS IN BULLDOG.

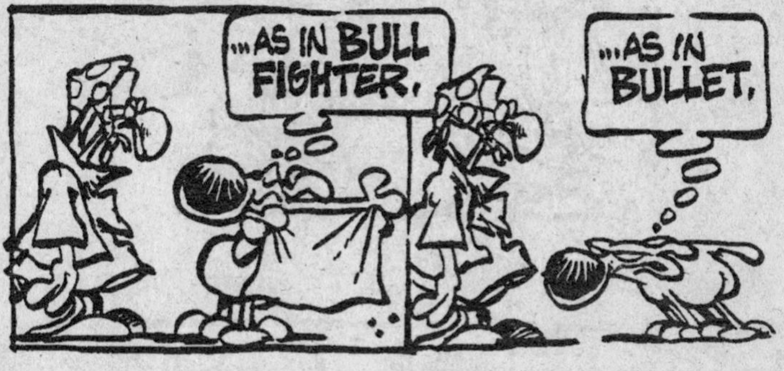
...AS IN BULL FIGHTER.
...AS IN BULLET.

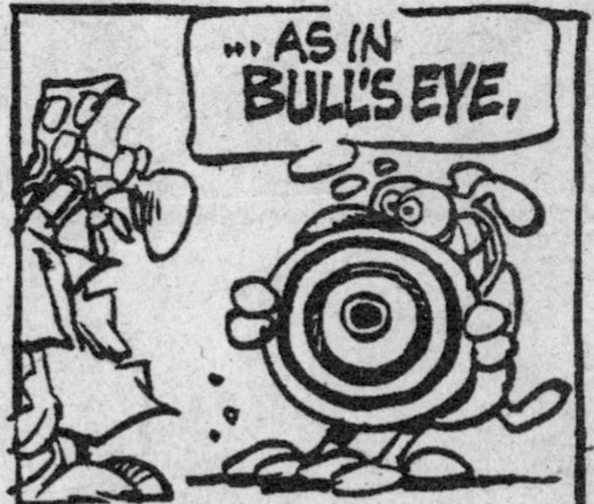
...AS IN BULL'S EYE.

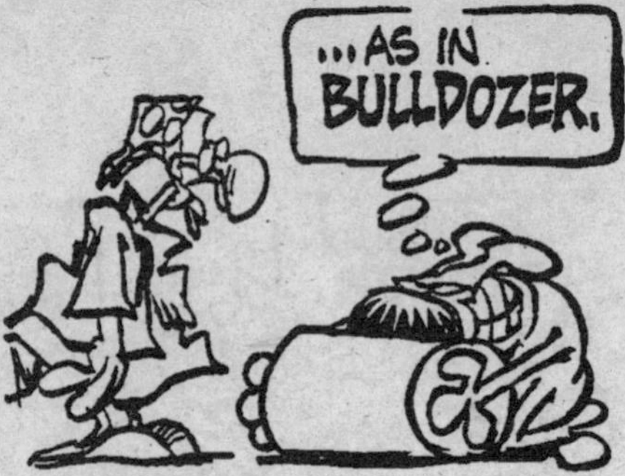
...AS IN BULLDOZER.

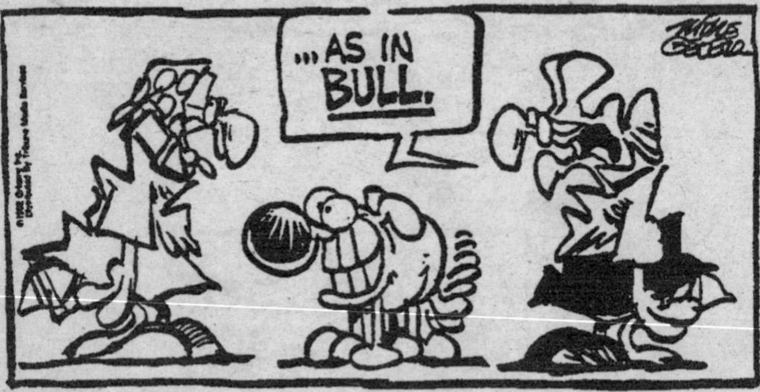
...AS IN BULL.

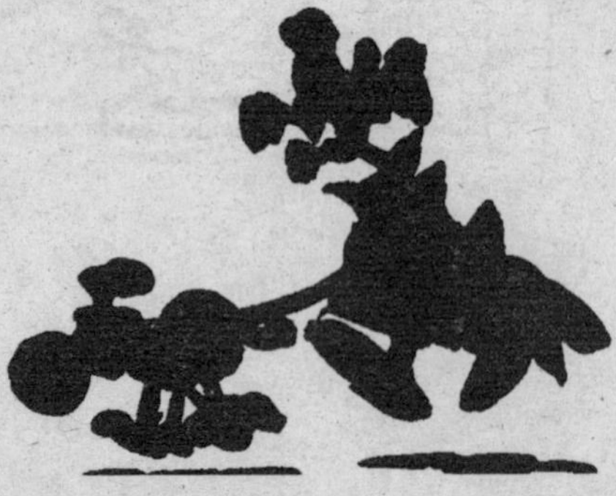

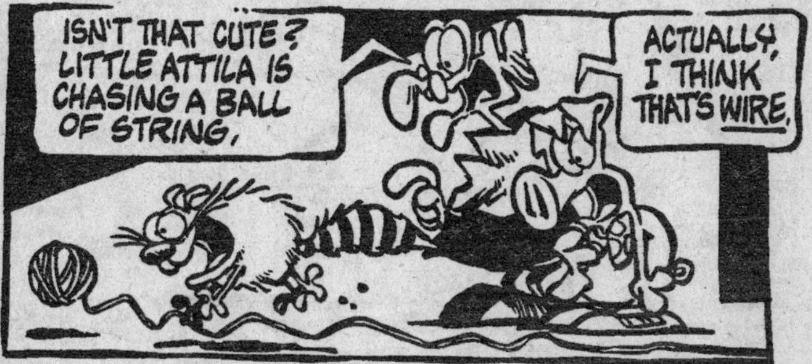
ISN'T THAT CUTE? LITTLE ATTILA IS CHASING A BALL OF STRING.
ACTUALLY, I THINK THAT'S WIRE.

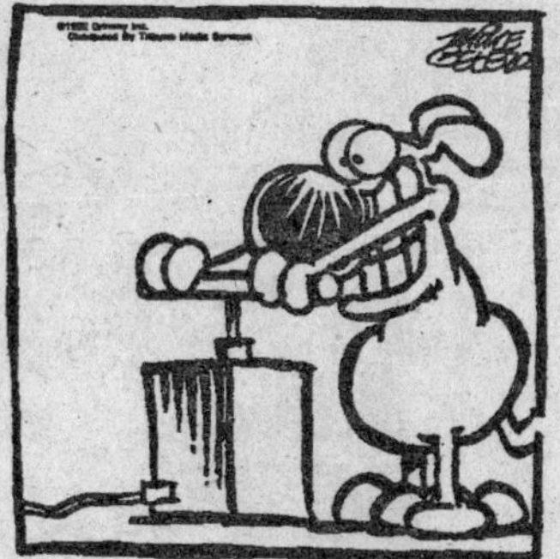

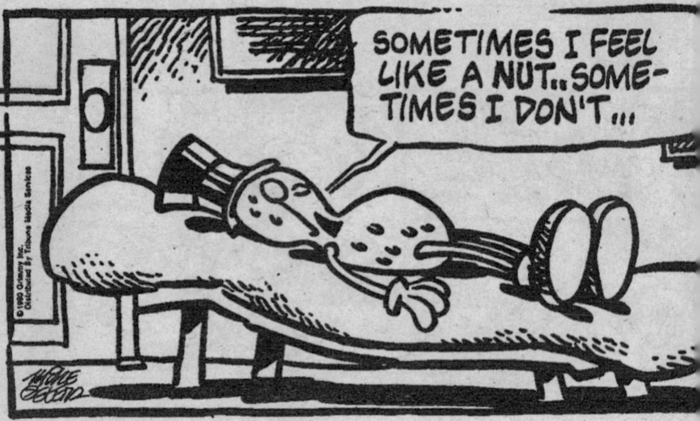
SOMETIMES I FEEL LIKE A NUT.. SOME-TIMES I DON'T...
© 1990 Grimmy Inc. Distributed By Tribune Media Services

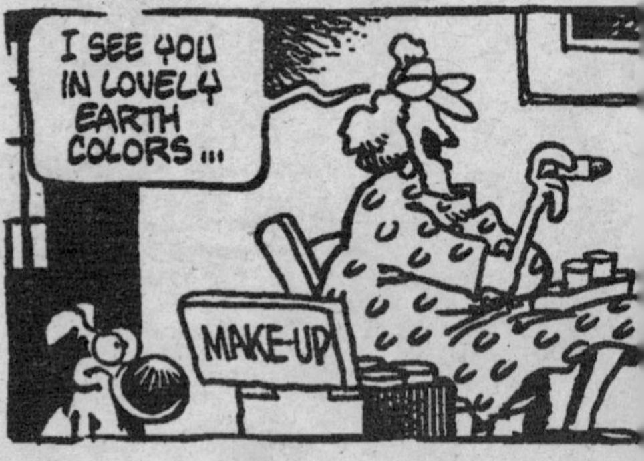
I SEE YOU IN LOVELY EARTH COLORS...
MAKE-UP

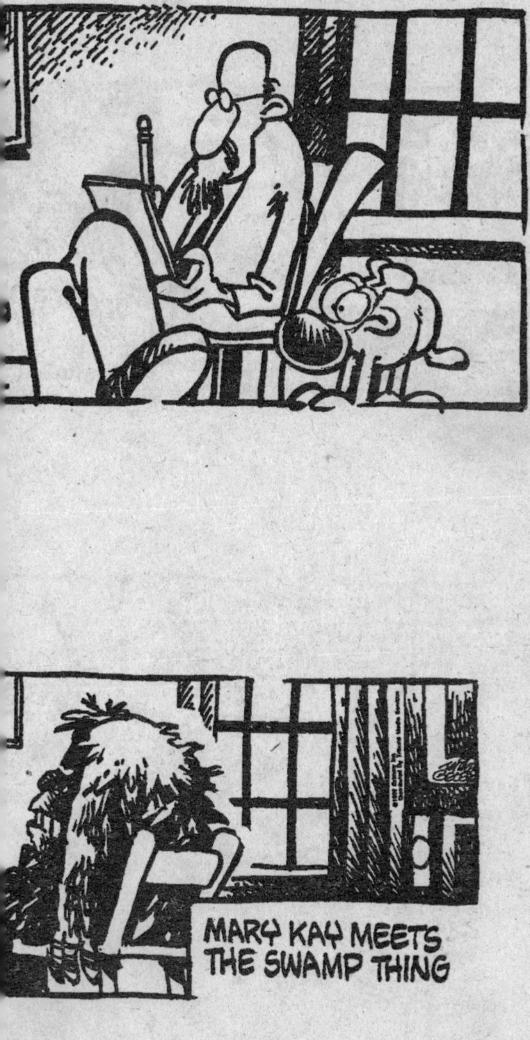
MARY KAY MEETS
THE SWAMP THING

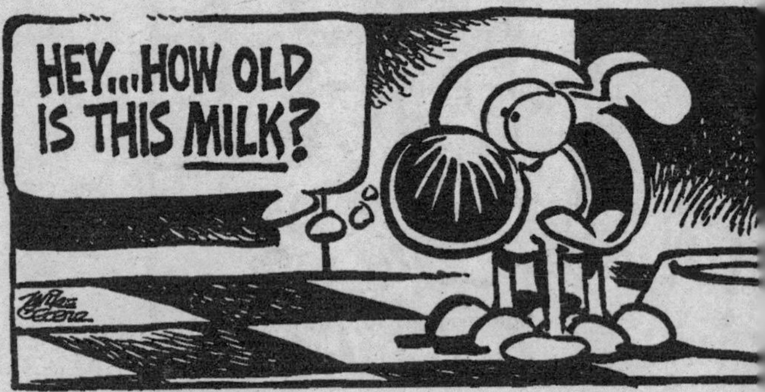
HEY...HOW OLD IS THIS MILK?

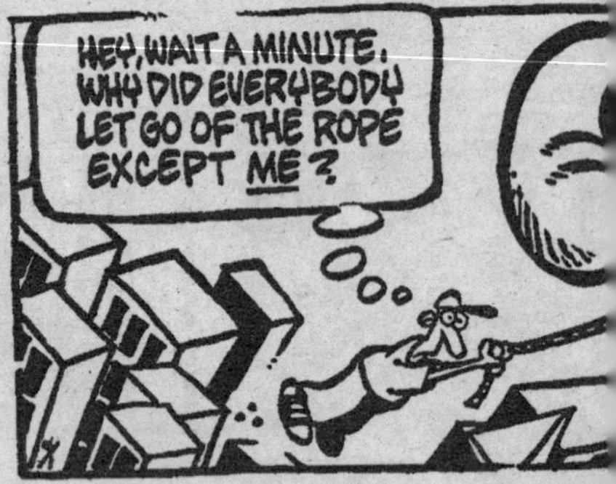
HEY, WAIT A MINUTE. WHY DID EVERYBODY LET GO OF THE ROPE EXCEPT ME?

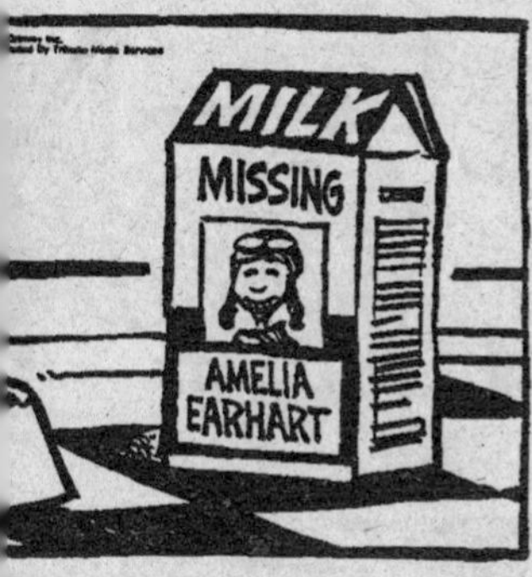
MILK
MISSING
AMELIA EARHART

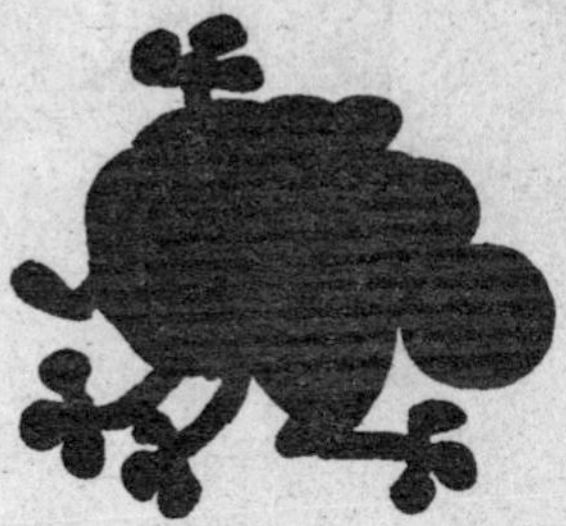

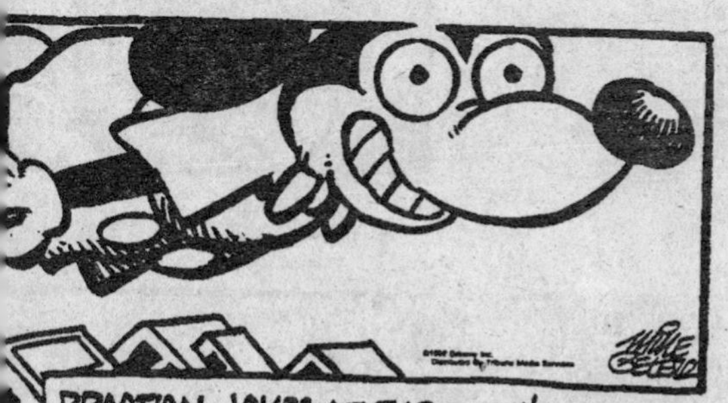

PRACTICAL JOKES AT THE MACY'S PARADE

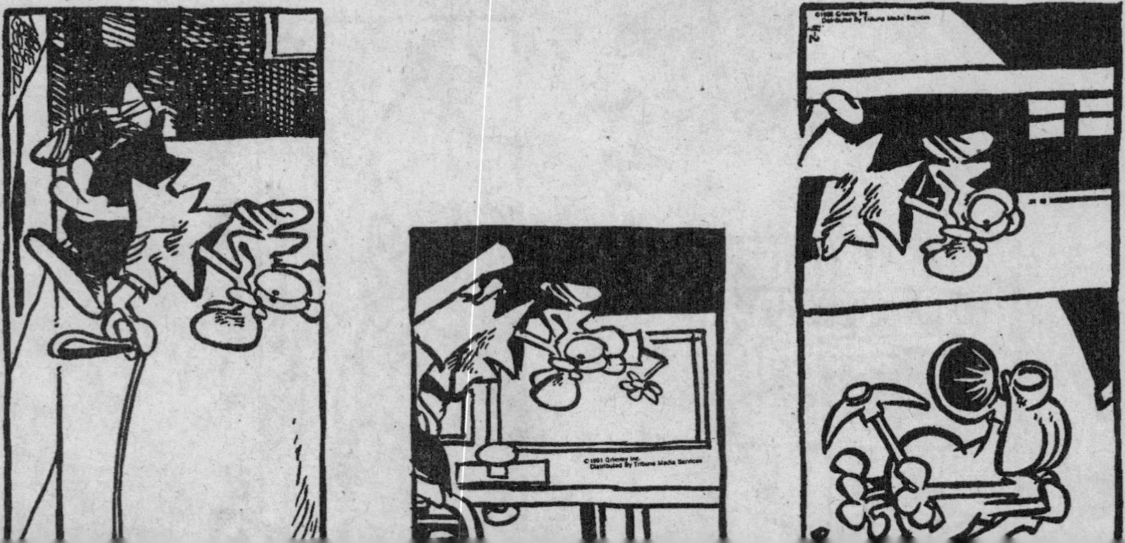
©1991 Grimmy Inc.
Distributed By Tribune Media Services

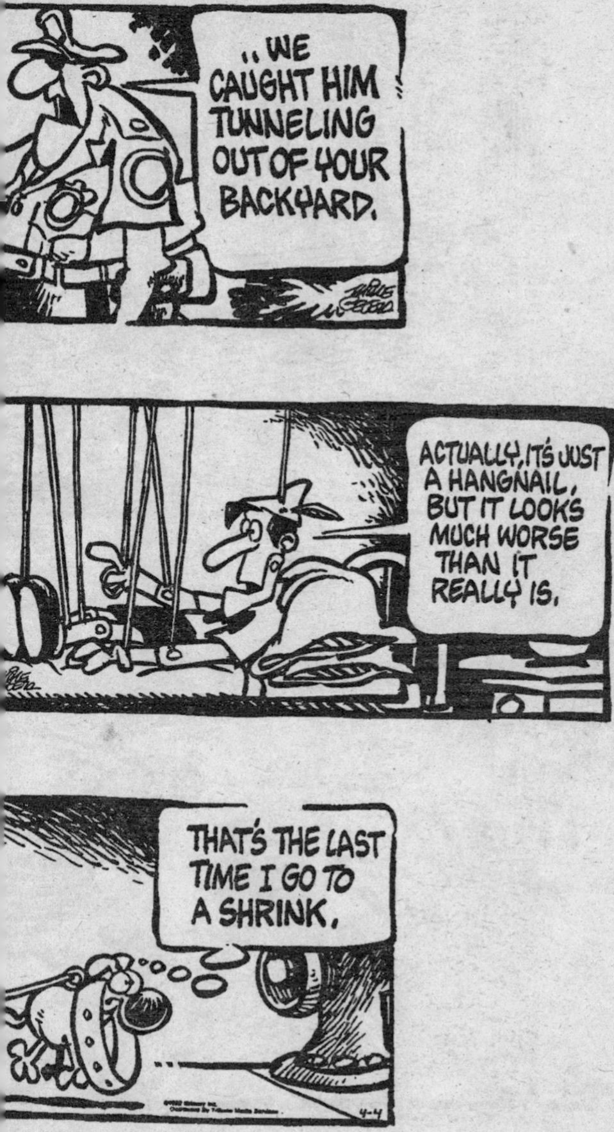
.. WE CAUGHT HIM TUNNELING OUT OF YOUR BACKYARD.
ACTUALLY, IT'S JUST A HANGNAIL, BUT IT LOOKS MUCH WORSE THAN IT REALLY IS.
THAT'S THE LAST TIME I GO TO A SHRINK.
4-4

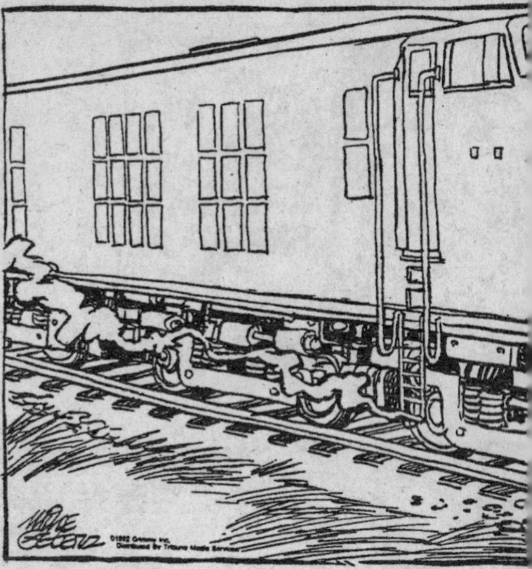
©1992 Grimmy Inc.
Distributed By Tribune Media Services

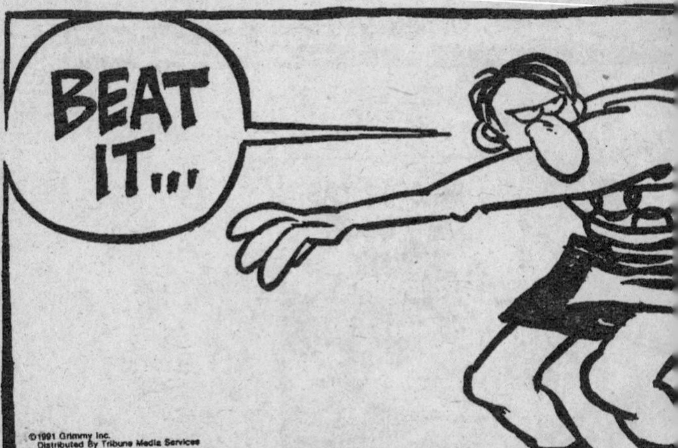
BEAT IT...
©1991 Grimmy Inc.
Distributed By Tribune Media Services

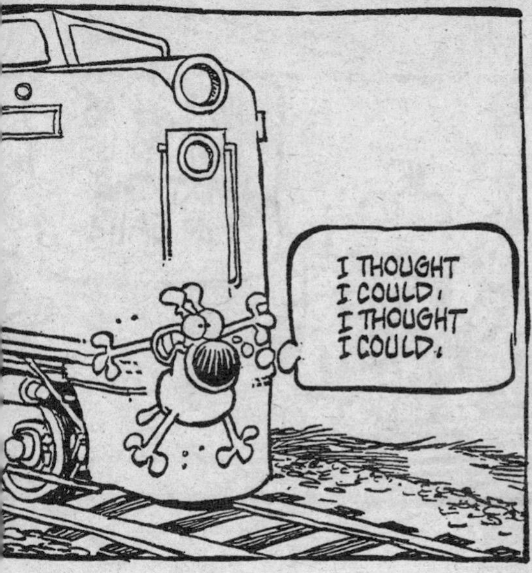
I THOUGHT I COULD, I THOUGHT I COULD.

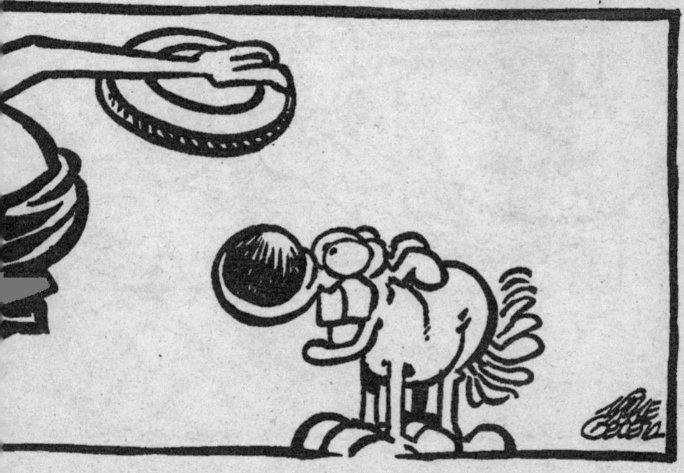

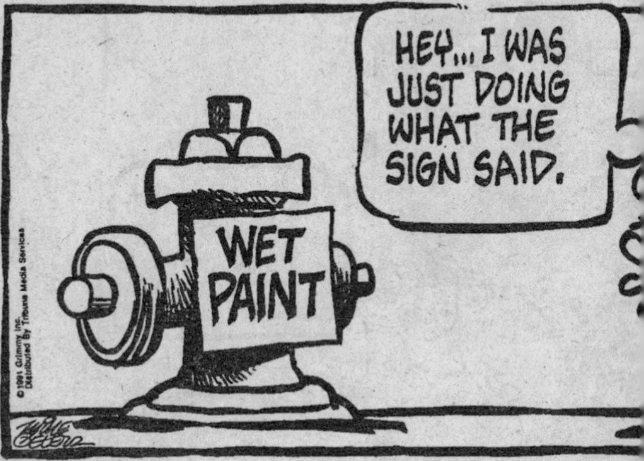
WET PAINT
HEY... I WAS JUST DOING WHAT THE SIGN SAID.
© 1991 Grimmy Inc. Distributed By Tribune Media Services

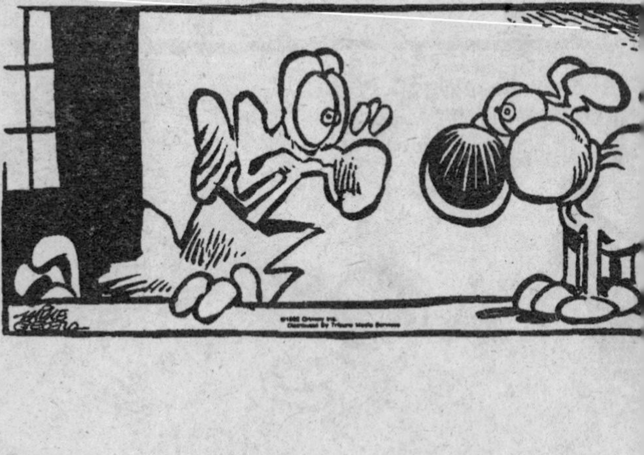

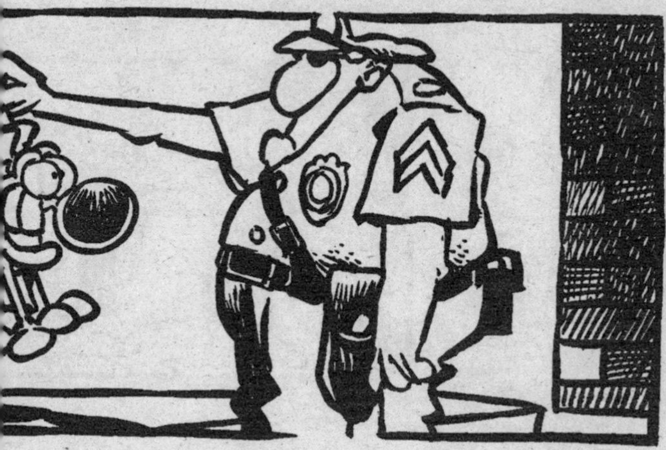

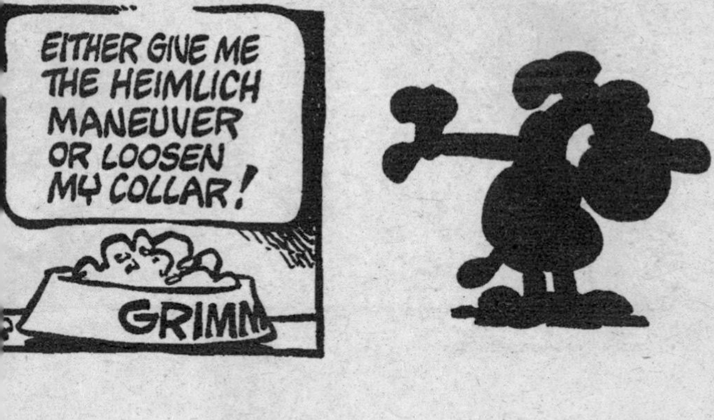
EITHER GIVE ME THE HEIMLICH MANEUVER OR LOOSEN MY COLLAR!
GRIMM

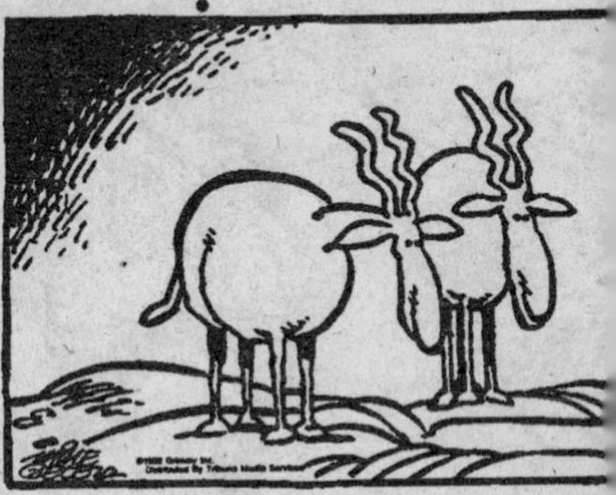

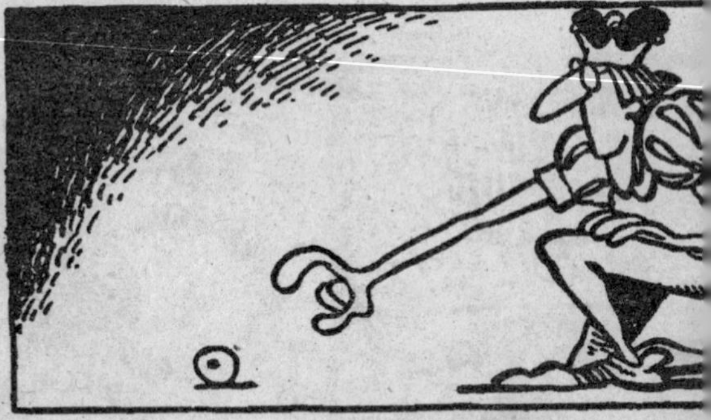

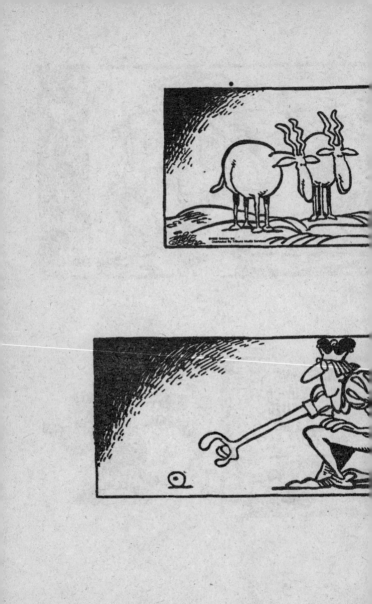

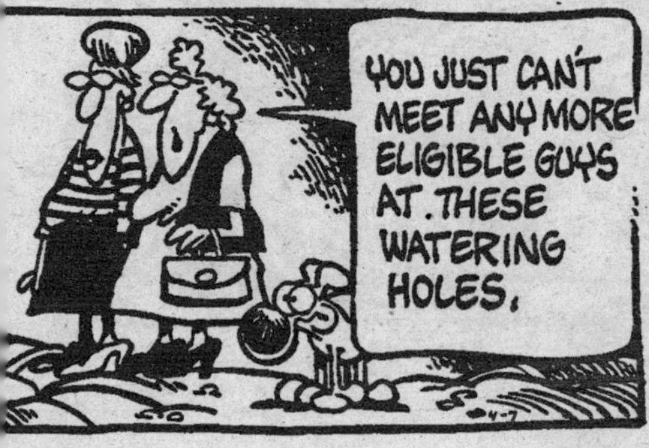
YOU JUST CAN'T MEET ANY MORE ELIGIBLE GUYS AT THESE WATERING HOLES.
4-7

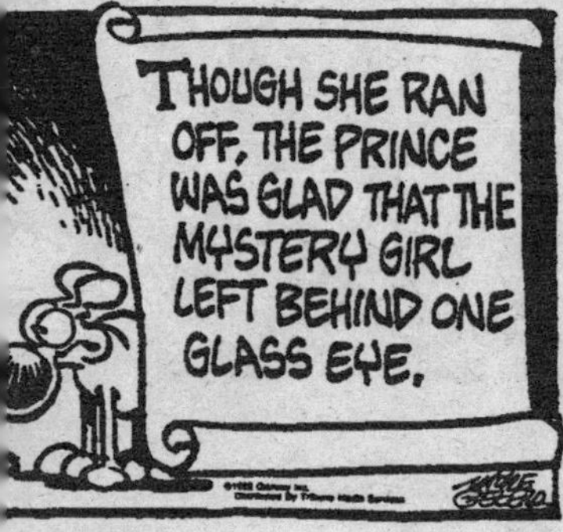
THOUGH SHE RAN OFF, THE PRINCE WAS GLAD THAT THE MYSTERY GIRL LEFT BEHIND ONE GLASS EYE.

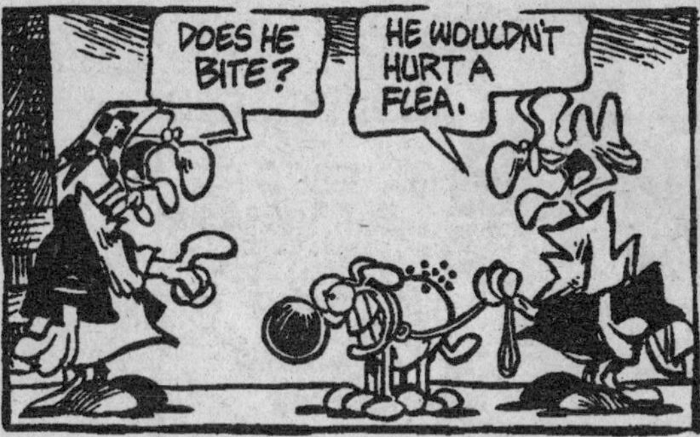
DOES HE BITE?
HE WOULDN'T HURT A FLEA.

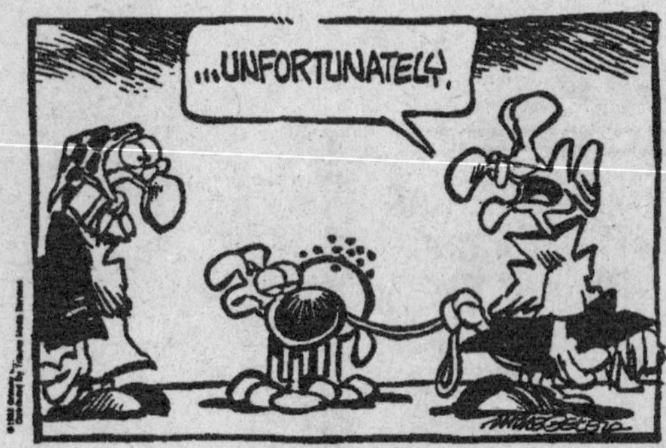
...UNFORTUNATELY.

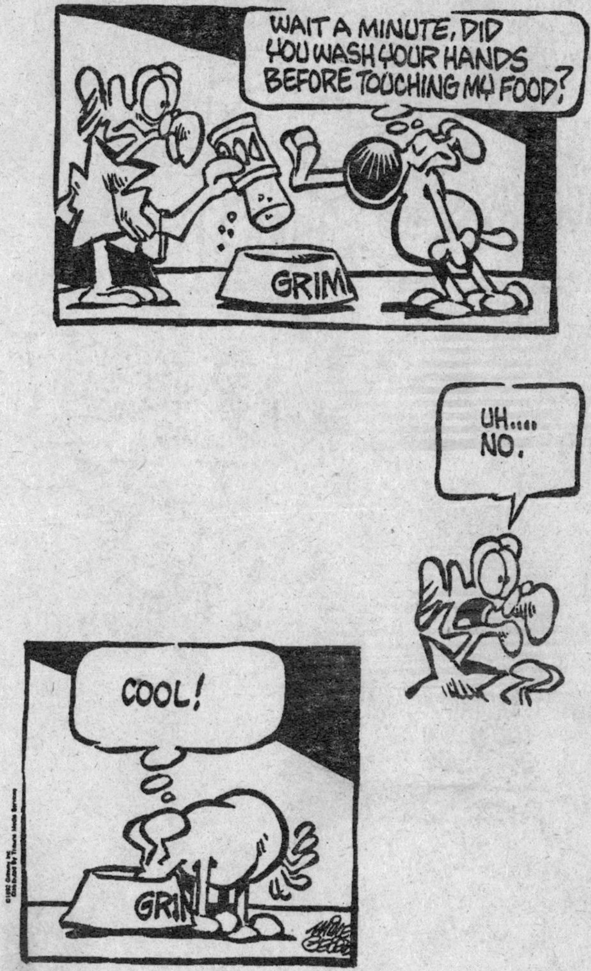
WAIT A MINUTE, DID YOU WASH YOUR HANDS BEFORE TOUCHING MY FOOD?
GRIM
UH.... NO.
COOL!
GRI

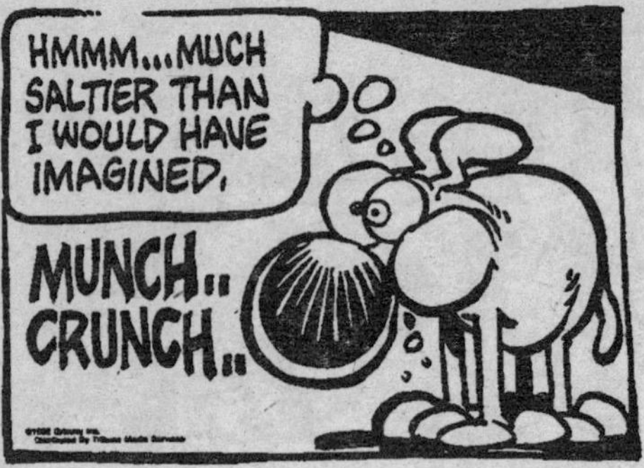
HMMM...MUCH SALTIER THAN I WOULD HAVE IMAGINED.
MUNCH.. CRUNCH..

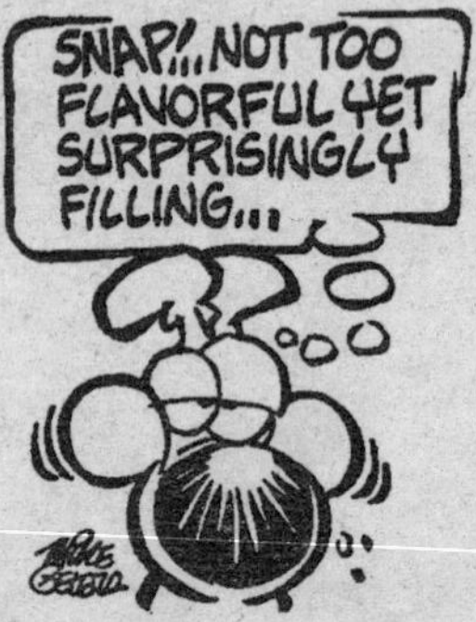
SNAP!...NOT TOO FLAVORFUL YET SURPRISINGLY FILLING...

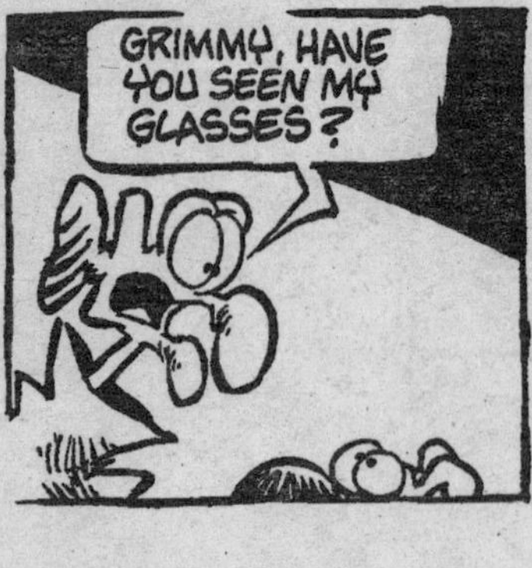
GRIMMY, HAVE YOU SEEN MY GLASSES?

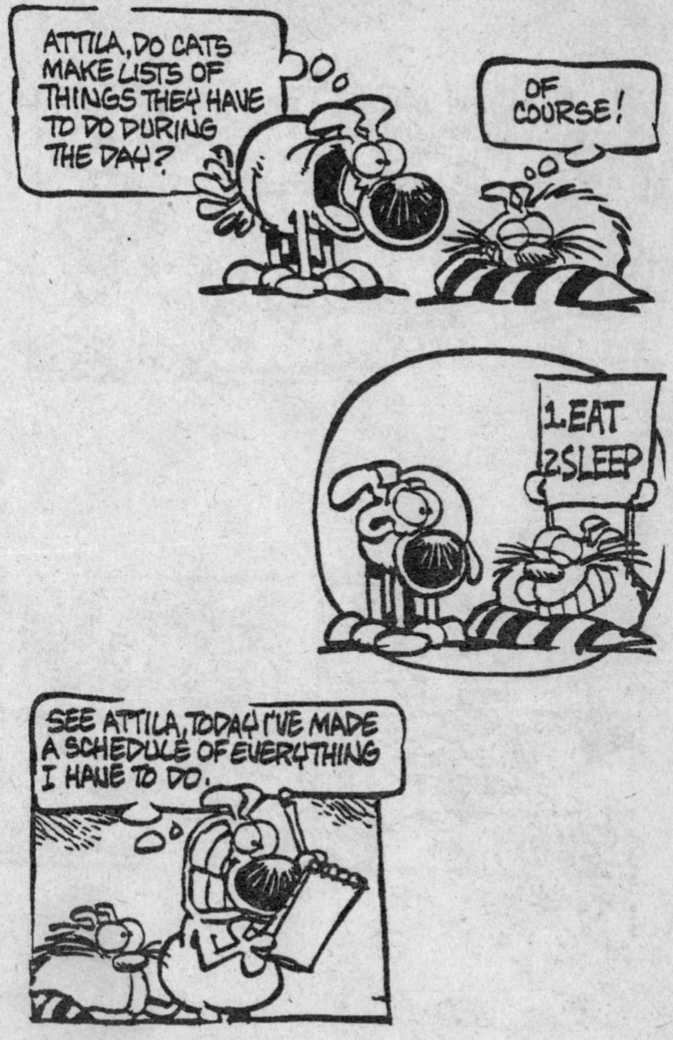
ATTILA, DO CATS MAKE LISTS OF THINGS THEY HAVE TO DO DURING THE DAY?
OF COURSE!
1. EAT
2. SLEEP
SEE ATTILA, TODAY I'VE MADE A SCHEDULE OF EVERYTHING I HAVE TO DO.

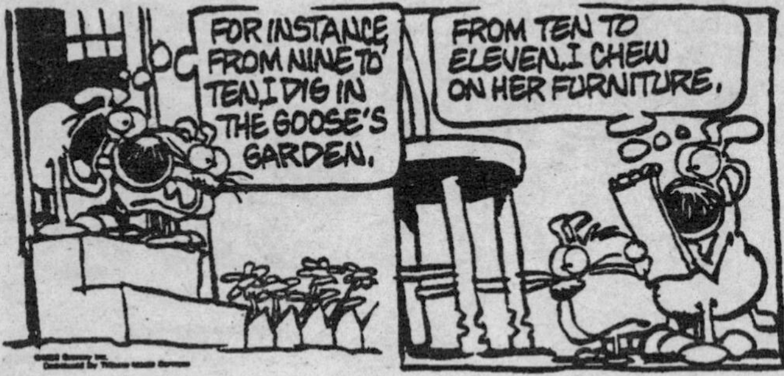
FOR INSTANCE, FROM NINE TO TEN, I DIG IN THE GOOSE'S GARDEN.
FROM TEN TO ELEVEN, I CHEW ON HER FURNITURE.

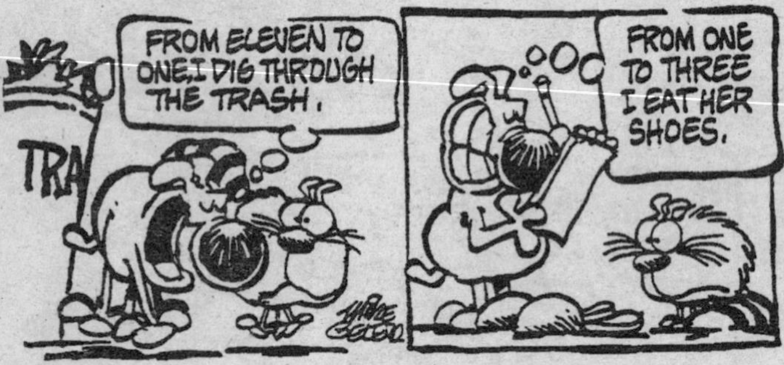
FROM ELEVEN TO ONE, I DIG THROUGH THE TRASH.
TRA
FROM ONE TO THREE I EAT HER SHOES.

FROM THREE TO FOUR I SHRED HER NEWSPAPER.
AND AT FOUR I CHEW UP HER ORIENTAL RUG.
WHAT DO YOU DO AT FIVE?
I JOIN THE WITNESS PROTECTION PROGRAM.

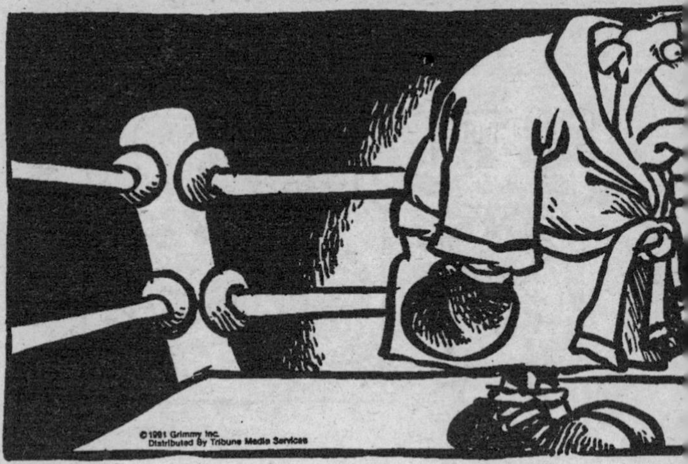
©1991 Grimmy Inc.
Distributed By Tribune Media Services

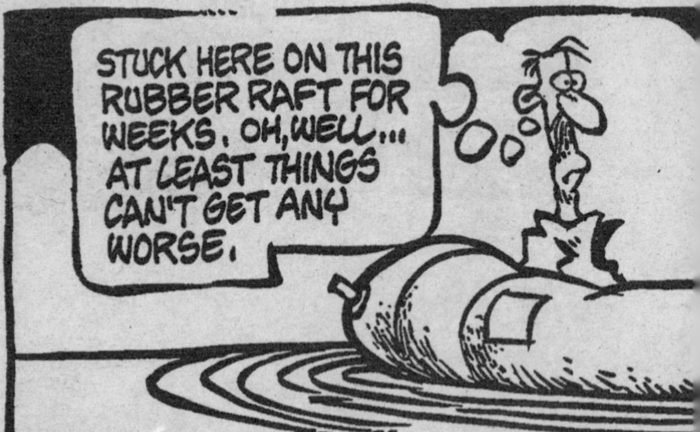
STUCK HERE ON THIS RUBBER RAFT FOR WEEKS. OH, WELL... AT LEAST THINGS CAN'T GET ANY WORSE.

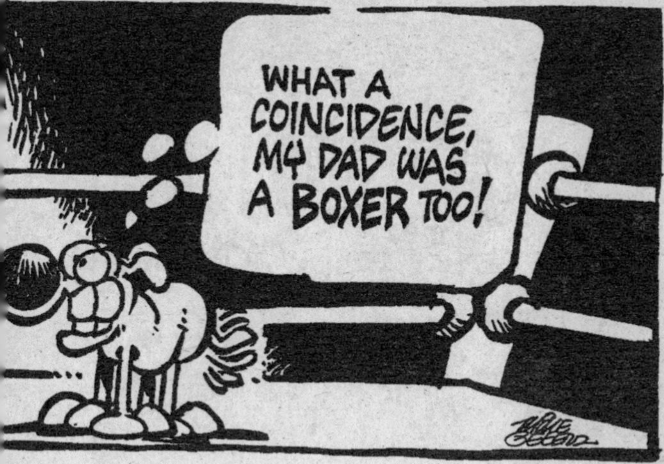
WHAT A COINCIDENCE, MY DAD WAS A BOXER TOO!

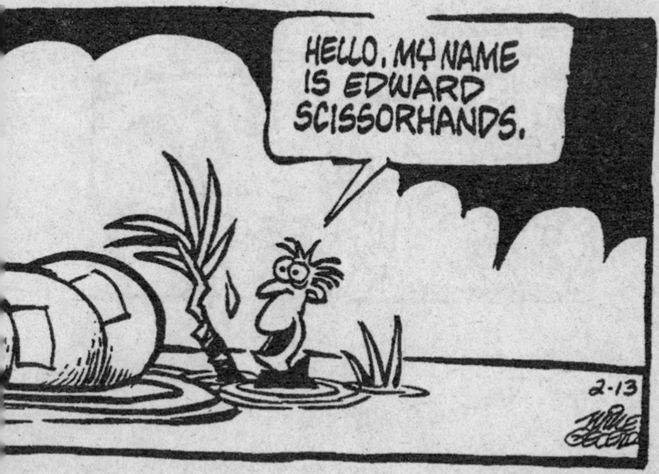
HELLO. MY NAME IS EDWARD SCISSORHANDS.
2-13

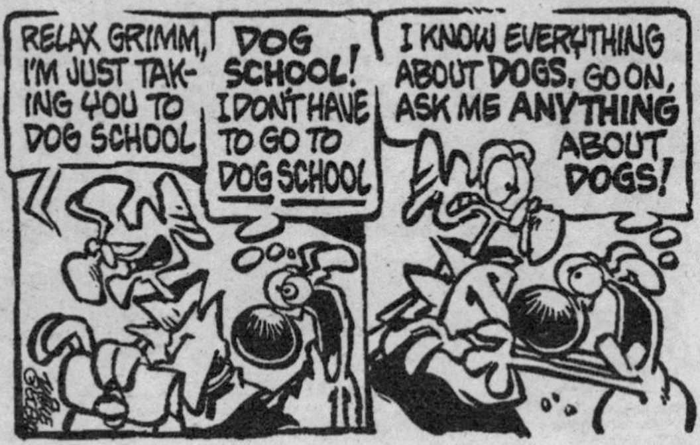
RELAX GRIMM, I'M JUST TAK-ING YOU TO DOG SCHOOL
DOG SCHOOL! I DON'T HAVE TO GO TO DOG SCHOOL
I KNOW EVERYTHING ABOUT DOGS, GO ON, ASK ME ANYTHING ABOUT DOGS!

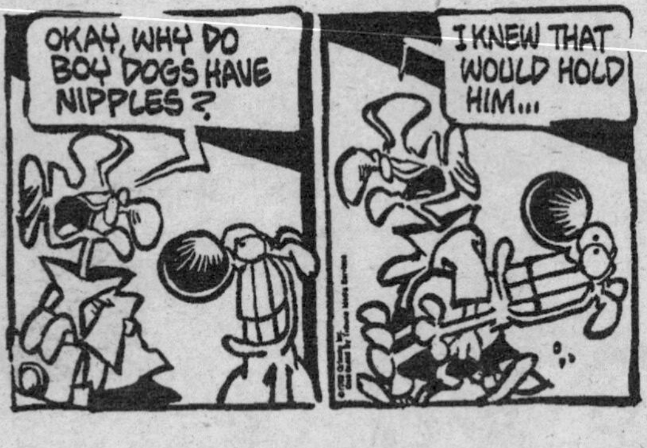
OKAY, WHY DO BOY DOGS HAVE NIPPLES?
I KNEW THAT WOULD HOLD HIM...

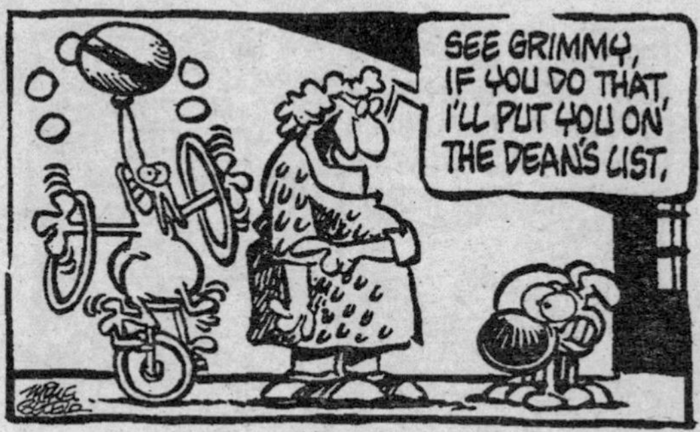
SEE GRIMMY, IF YOU DO THAT, I'LL PUT YOU ON THE DEAN'S LIST.

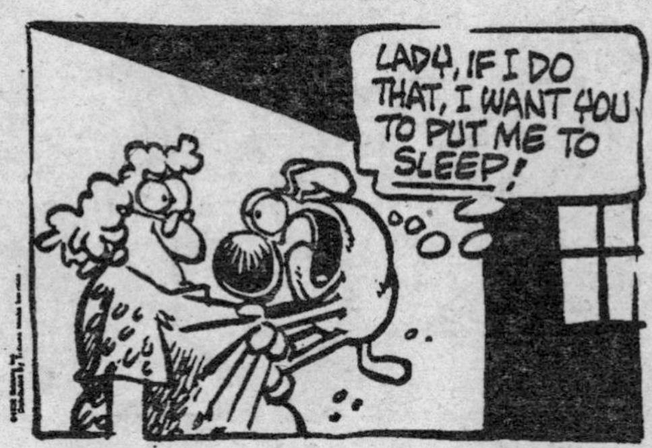
LADY, IF I DO THAT, I WANT YOU TO PUT ME TO SLEEP!

GRIMMY, I'M GOING TO USE HYPNOSIS TO STOP YOU FROM DRINKING OUT OF THE TOILET.
LOOK IN TO MY EYES AND REPEAT AFTER ME. "I WILL DO AS YOU SAY."
YOU WILL DO AS I SAY...
I WILL DO AS YOU SAY...
YOU WILL DO AS I SAY.
GLUG GLUG GLUG
GOOD, NOW LET'S SEE YOU CATCH A FRISBEE.

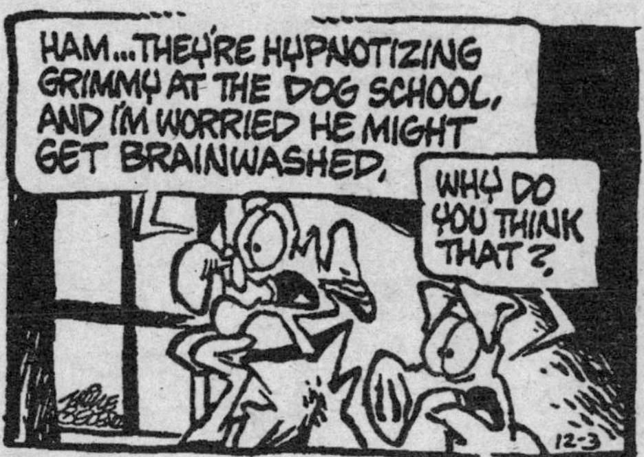
HAM...THEY'RE HYPNOTIZING GRIMMY AT THE DOG SCHOOL, AND I'M WORRIED HE MIGHT GET BRAINWASHED.
WHY DO YOU THINK THAT?
12-3

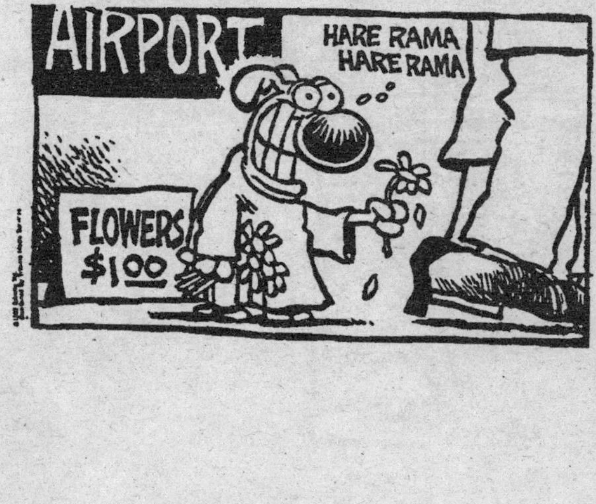
AIRPORT
HARE RAMA HARE RAMA
FLOWERS $1.00

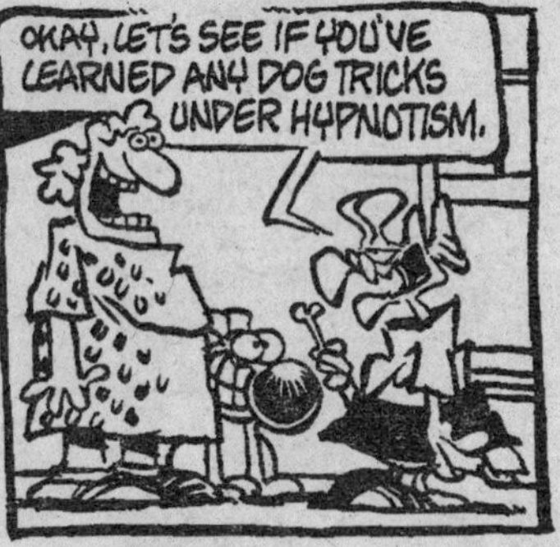
OKAY, LET'S SEE IF YOU'VE LEARNED ANY DOG TRICKS UNDER HYPNOTISM.

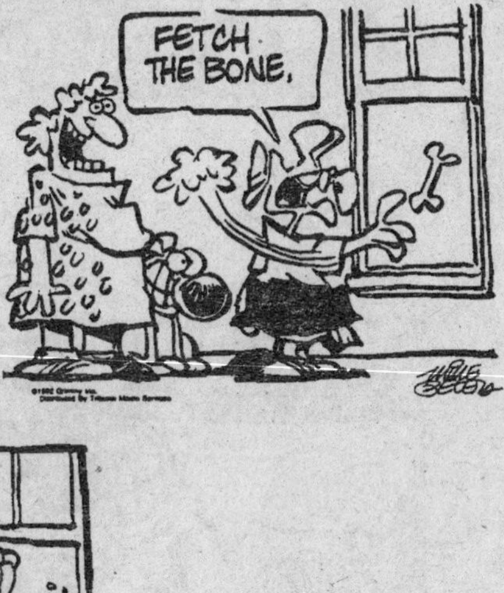
FETCH THE BONE.

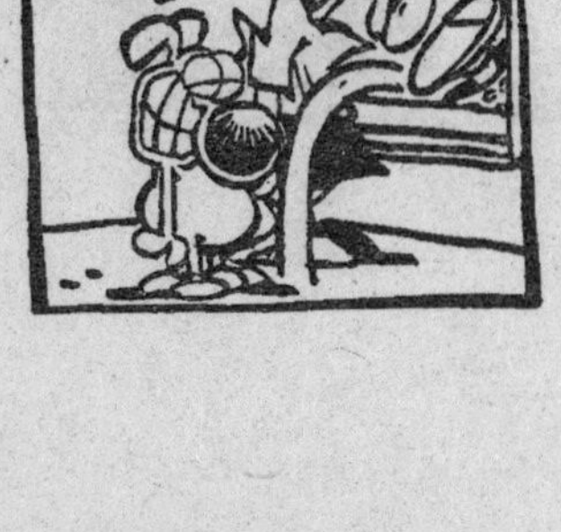
SHE'S GOOD ISN'T SHE?

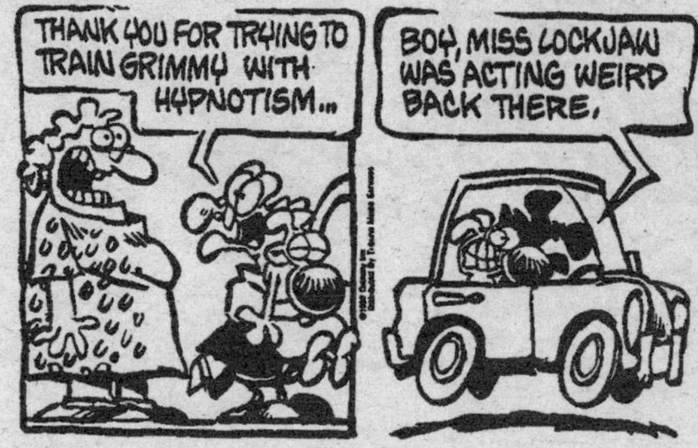
THANK YOU FOR TRYING TO TRAIN GRIMMY WITH HYPNOTISM...
BOY, MISS LOCKJAW WAS ACTING WEIRD BACK THERE.

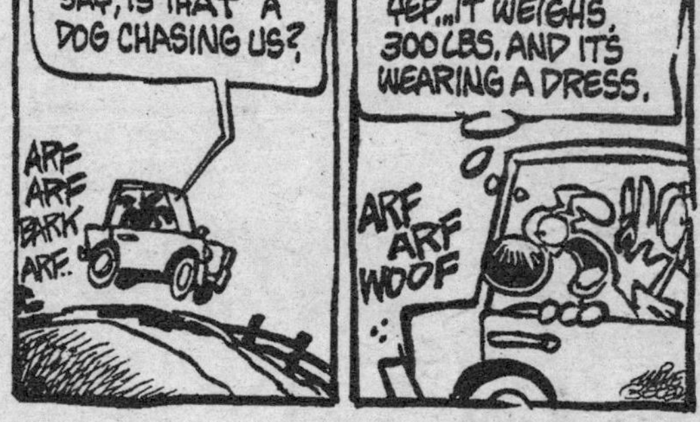
SAY, IS THAT A DOG CHASING US?
ARF ARF BARK ARF..
YEP...IT WEIGHS 300 LBS. AND IT'S WEARING A DRESS.
ARF ARF WOOF

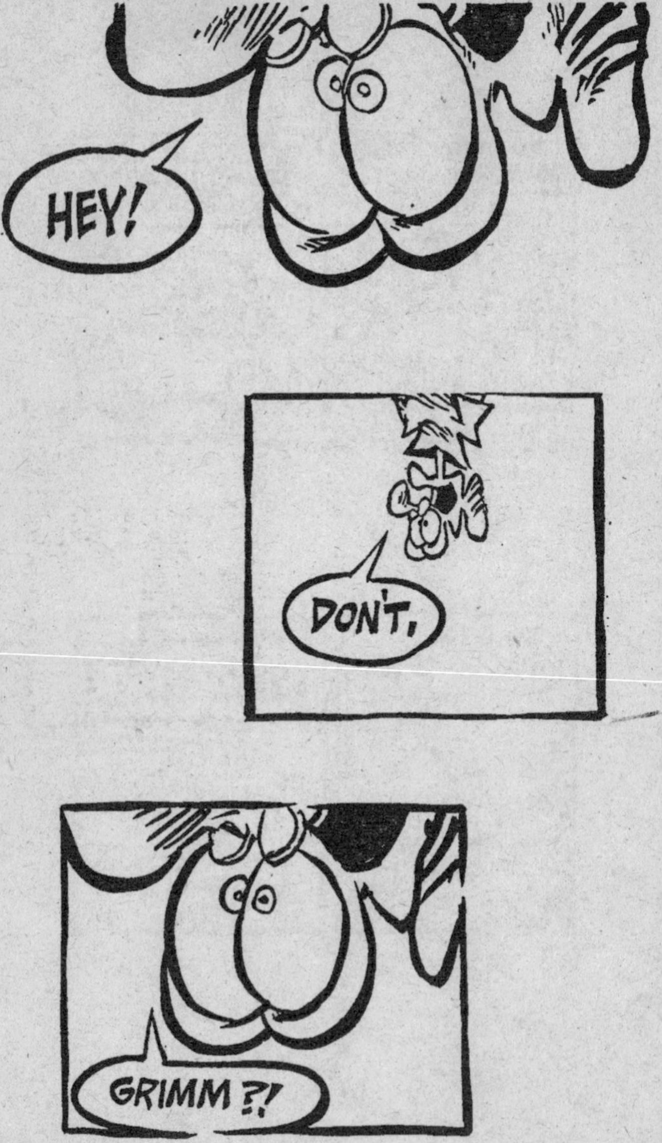
HEY!
DON'T.
GRIMM?!

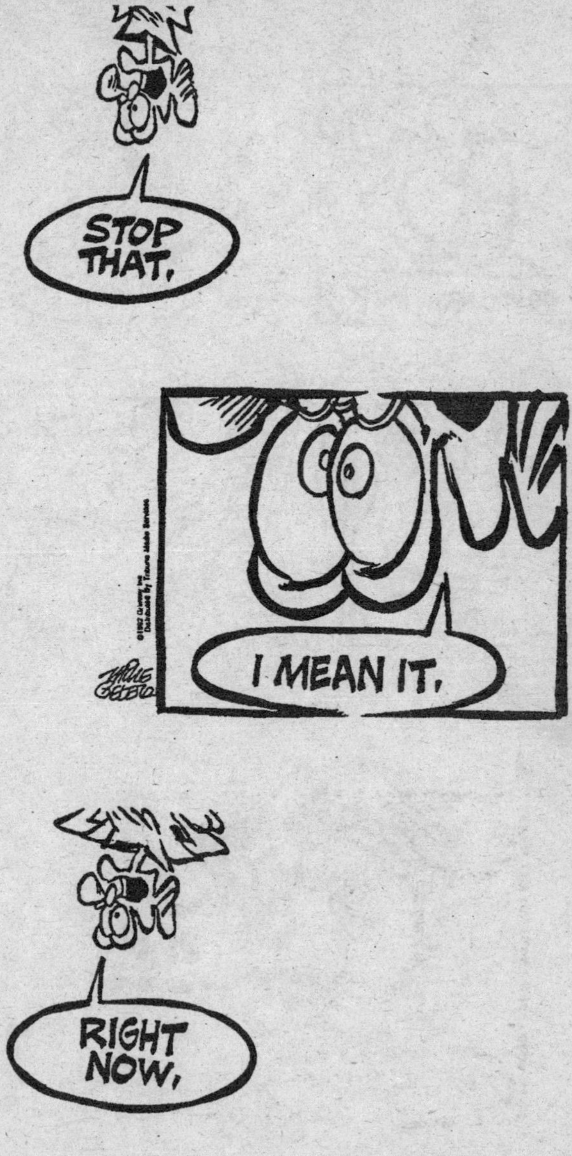
STOP THAT.
I MEAN IT.
RIGHT NOW.

DO YOU HEAR ME?
I'M SERIOUS.
STOP IT.
GRIMM...

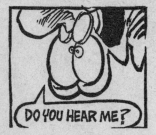

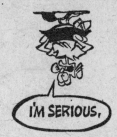

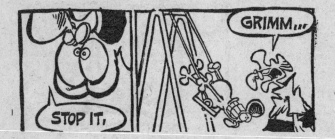

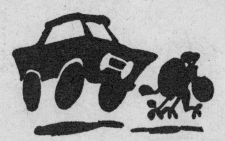

GEE... THIS SAYS THERE WAS A MAFIA TRIAL WHERE THE WHOLE JURY WAS FIXED.
3-24
OUCH! THAT HAD TO HURT.
WAYNE STAYSKAL

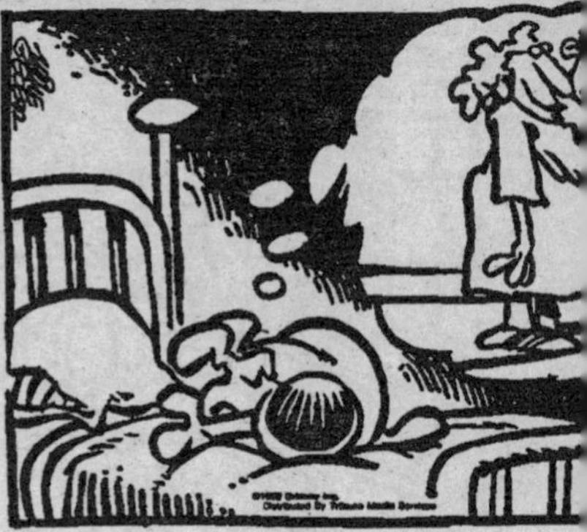

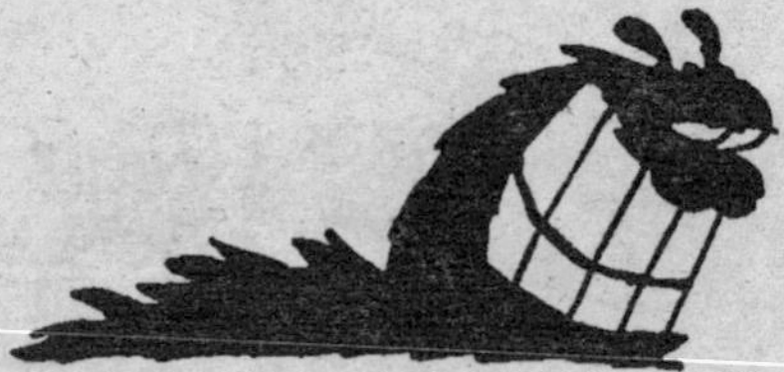

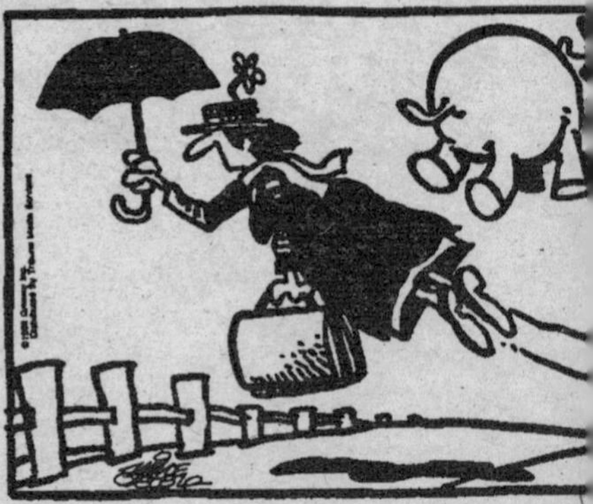

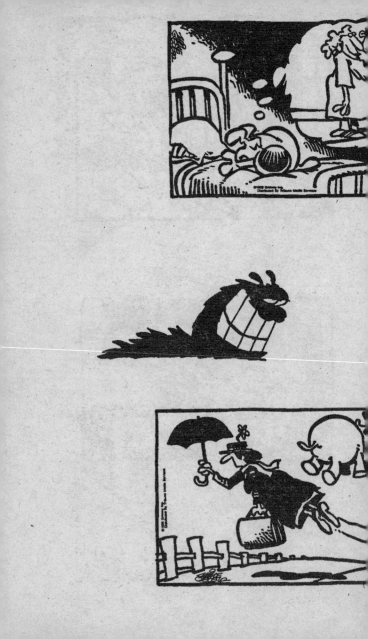

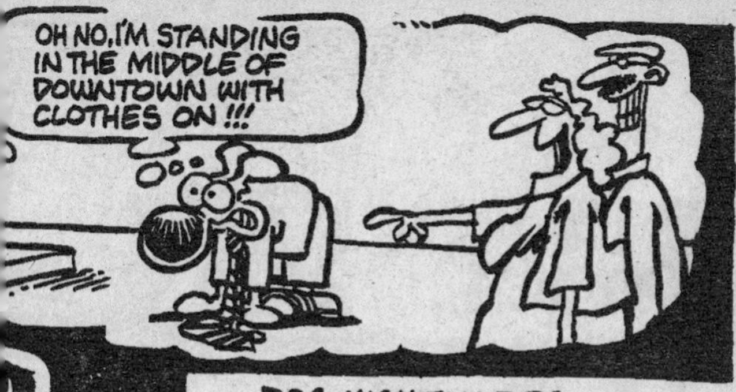
OH NO, I'M STANDING IN THE MIDDLE OF DOWNTOWN WITH CLOTHES ON !!!

DOG NIGHTMARES

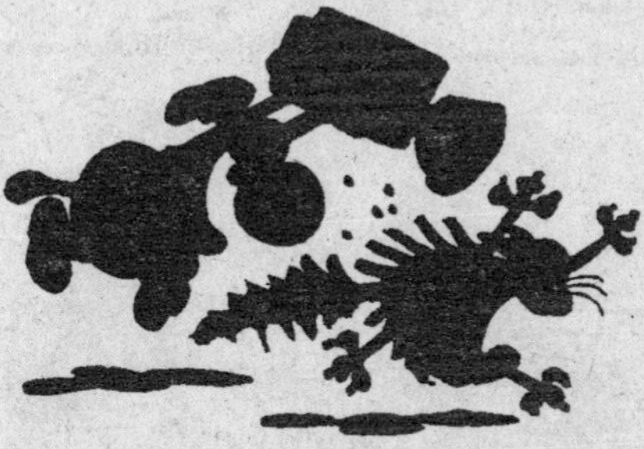

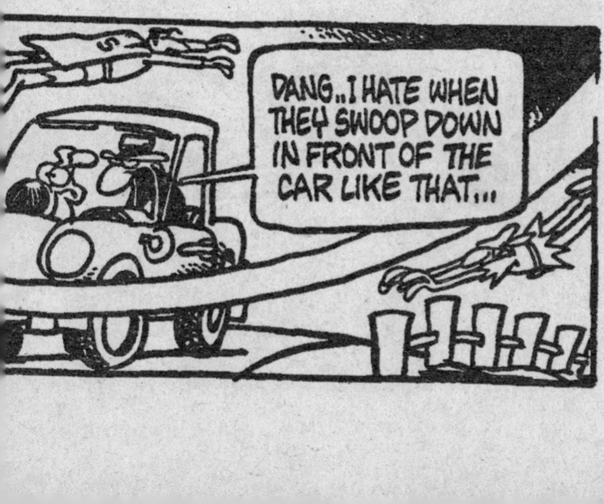
DANG.. I HATE WHEN THEY SWOOP DOWN IN FRONT OF THE CAR LIKE THAT...

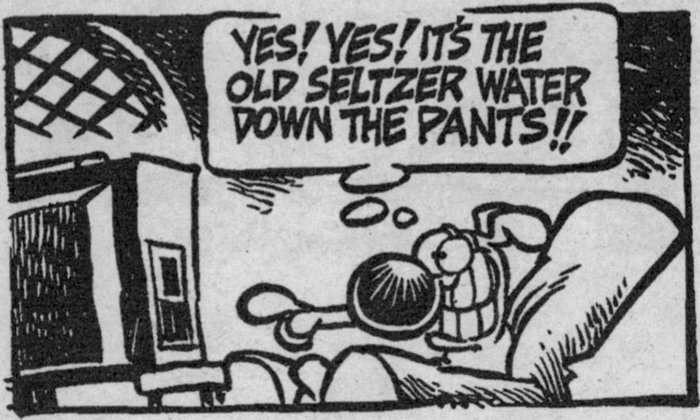
YES! YES! IT'S THE OLD SELTZER WATER DOWN THE PANTS!!

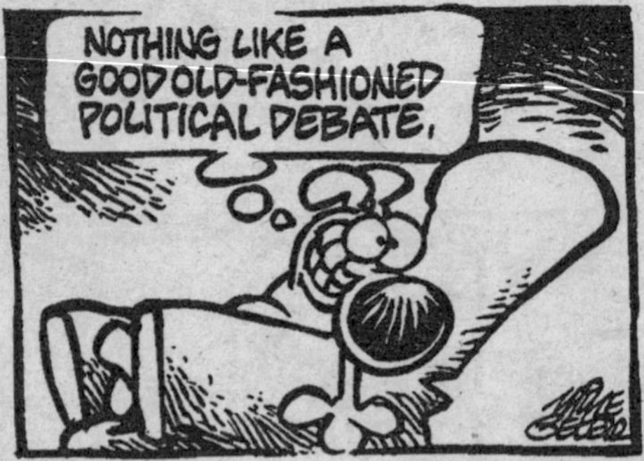
NOTHING LIKE A GOOD OLD-FASHIONED POLITICAL DEBATE.

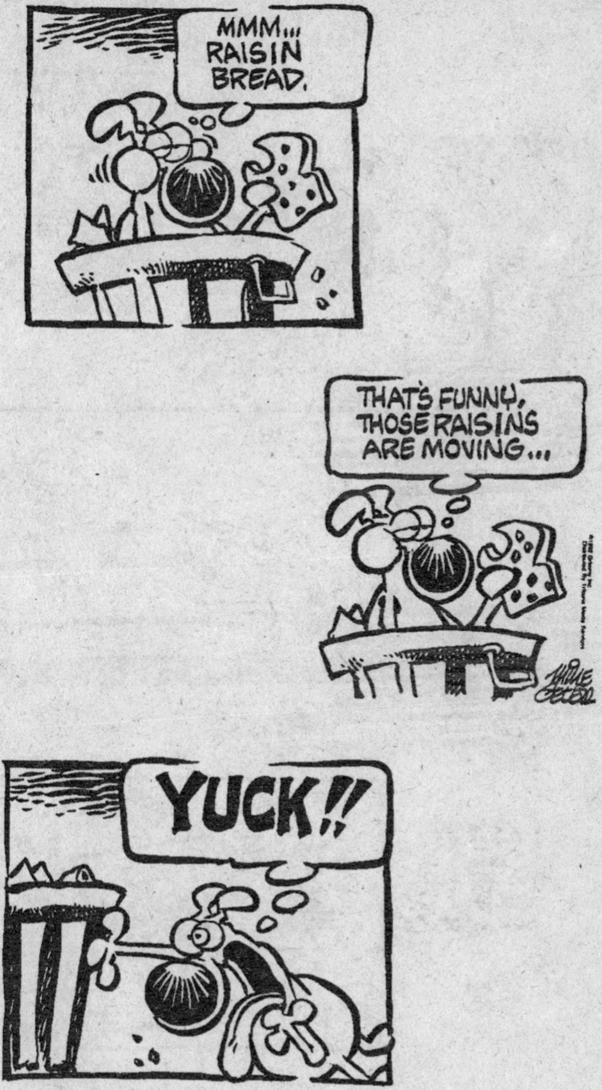
MMM... RAISIN BREAD.
THAT'S FUNNY, THOSE RAISINS ARE MOVING...
YUCK!!

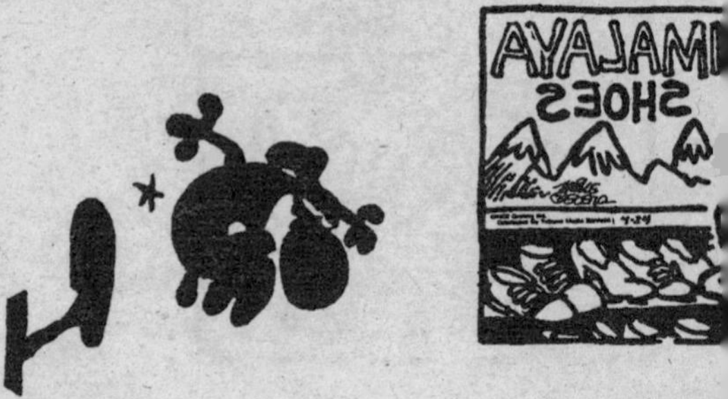
SHOES

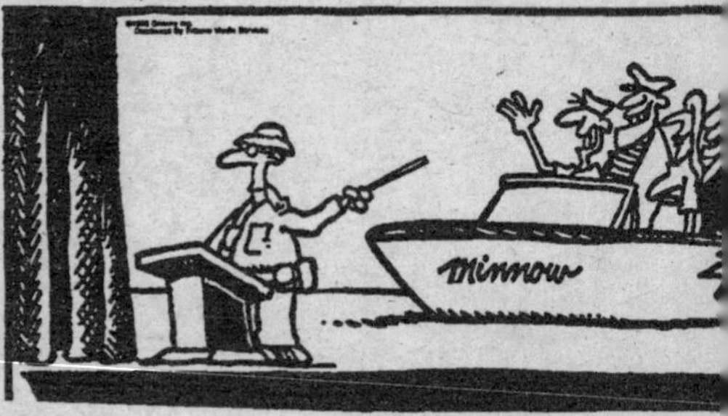
minnow

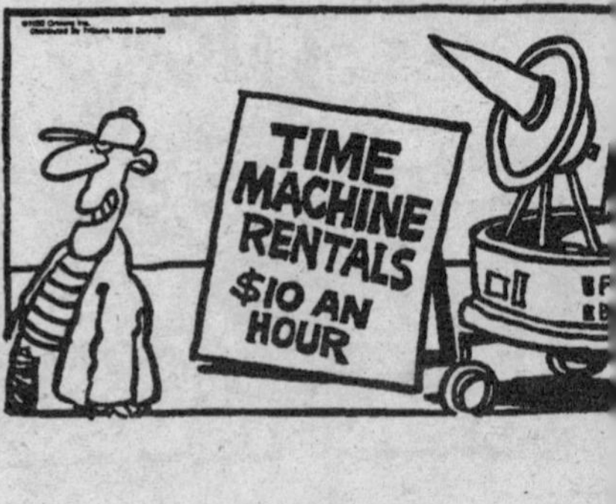
TIME MACHINE RENTALS
$10 AN HOUR

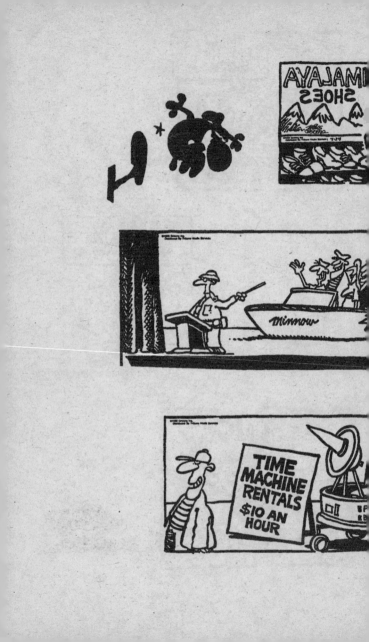

WHOA... 84-B! GEEZE, FELLA. YOU'VE GOT A BIG FOOT!! I MEAN A REEEALLY BIIIIG FOOT!

ALTHOUGH THE EXPEDITION TEAM COULD NOT FIND AMELIA EARHART, THEY DID LOCATE GILLIGAN, THE CAPTAIN AND THE CREW OF THE MINNOW.
5-1

DARN.. ANOTHER ONE CAME BACK BEFORE HE LEFT.

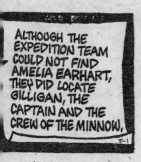

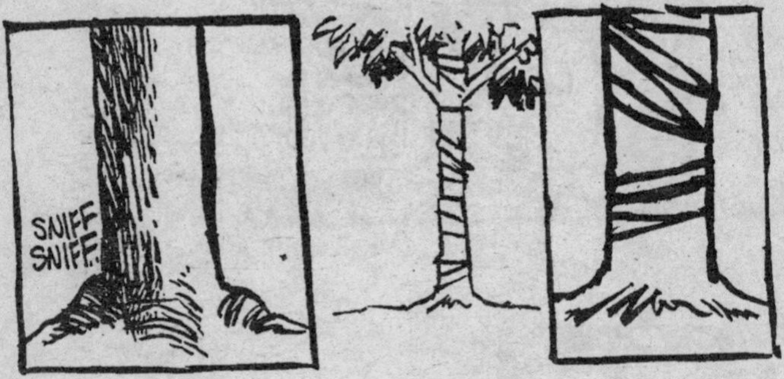
SNIFF SNIFF...

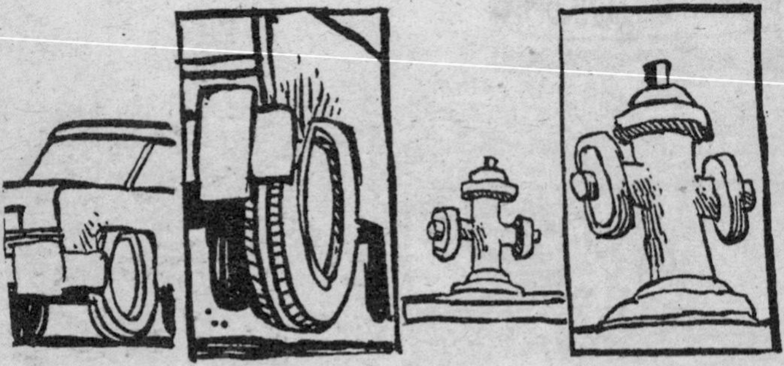

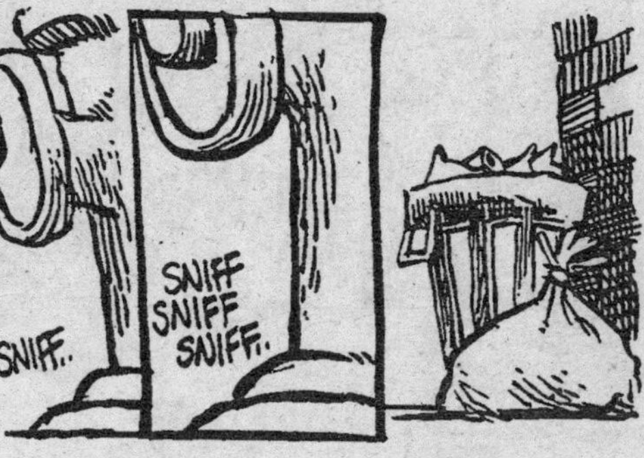
SNIFF..
SNIFF
SNIFF
SNIFF..

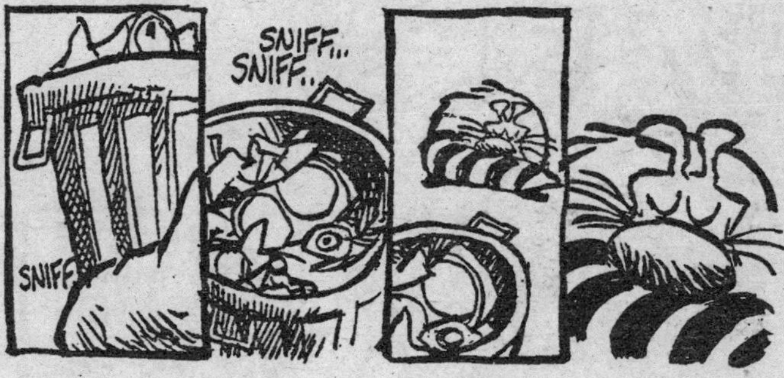
SNIFF
SNIFF...
SNIFF...

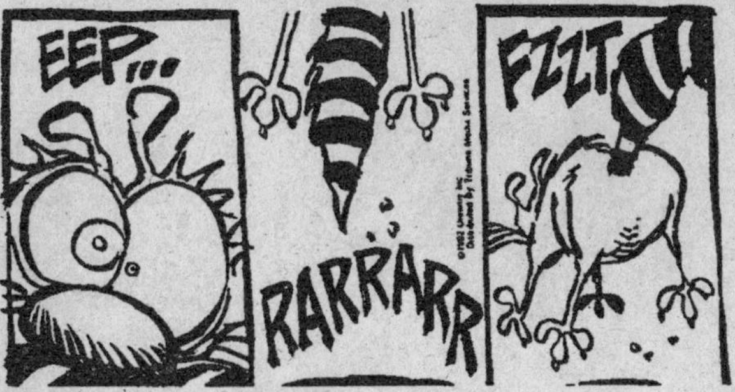
EEP...
RARRARR
FZZT

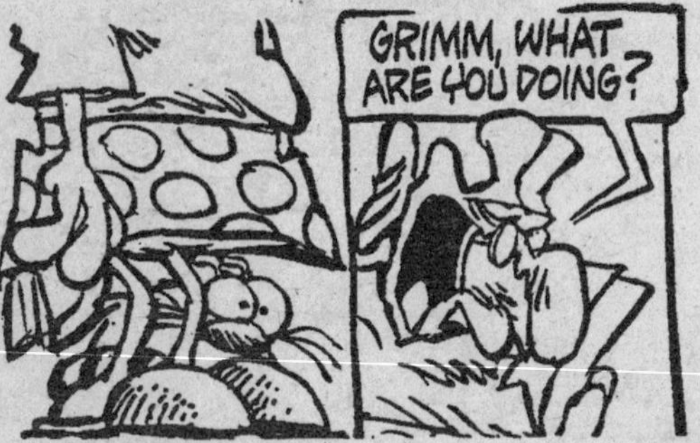
GRIMM, WHAT ARE YOU DOING?

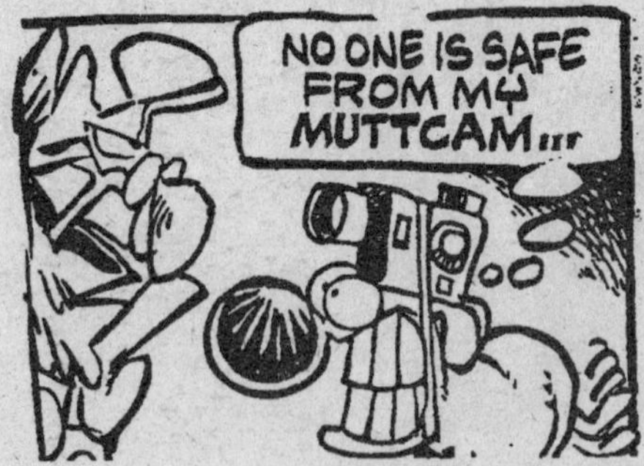
NO ONE IS SAFE FROM MY MUTTCAM...

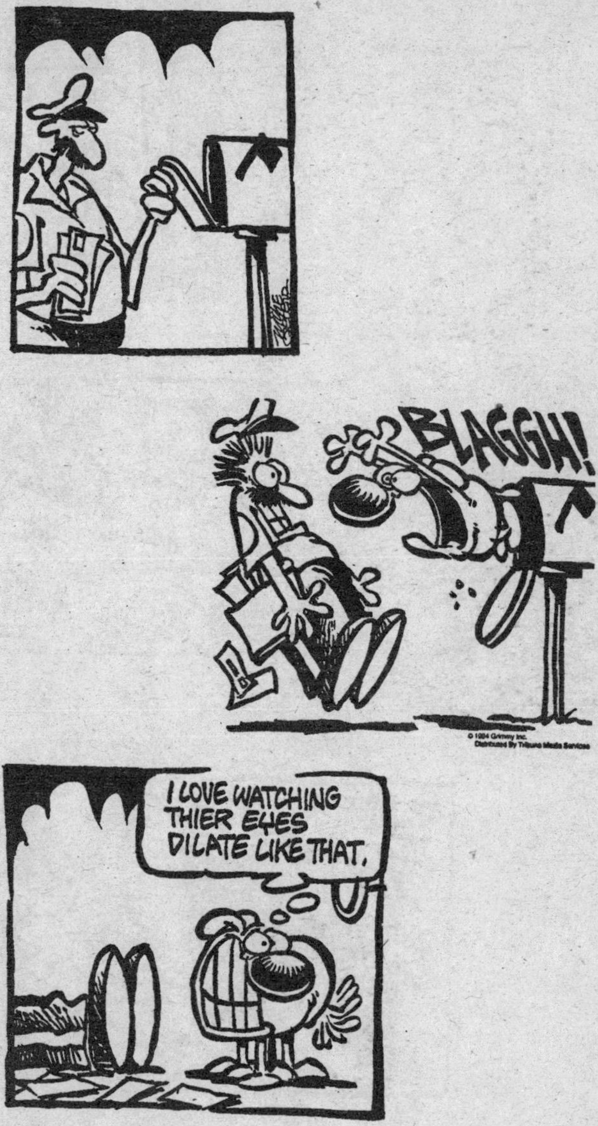
BLAGGH!
© 1994 Grimmy Inc.
Distributed By Tribune Media Services
I LOVE WATCHING THIER EYES DILATE LIKE THAT.

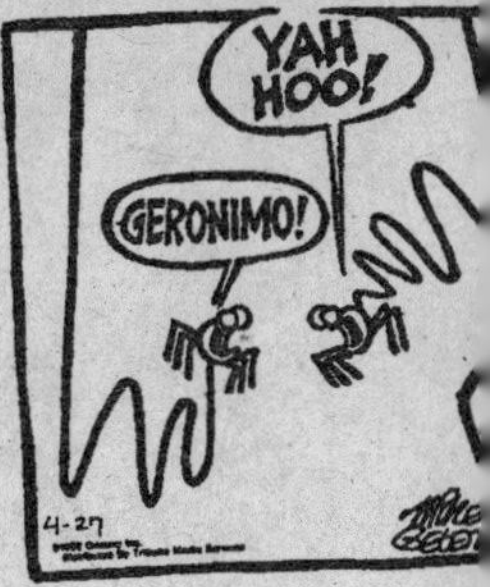
YAH HOO!
GERONIMO!
4-27

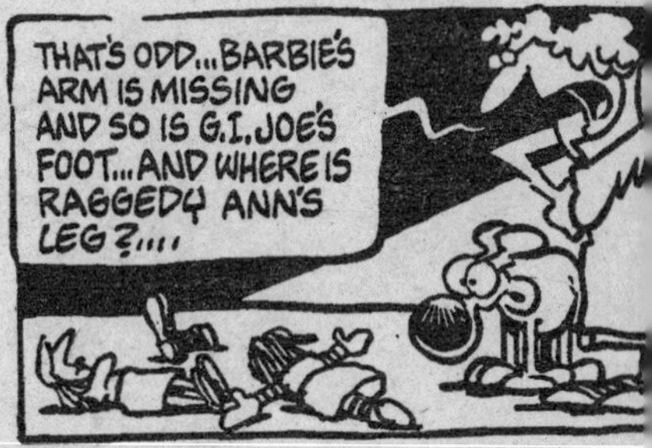
THAT'S ODD...BARBIE'S ARM IS MISSING AND SO IS G.I. JOE'S FOOT...AND WHERE IS RAGGEDY ANN'S LEG?....

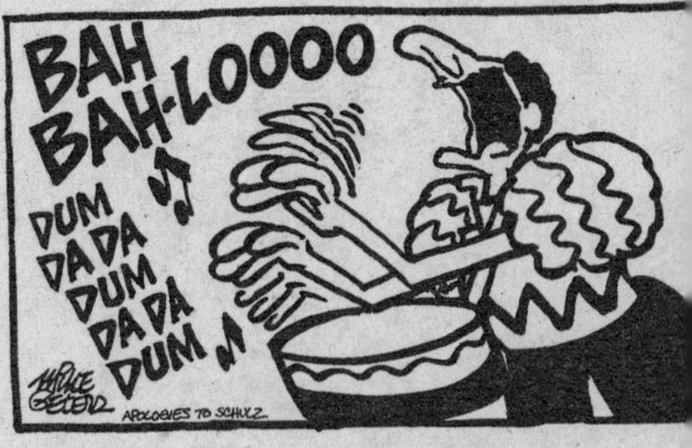
BAH BAH-LOOOO
DUM DA DA DUM DA DA DUM
APOLOGIES TO SCHULZ

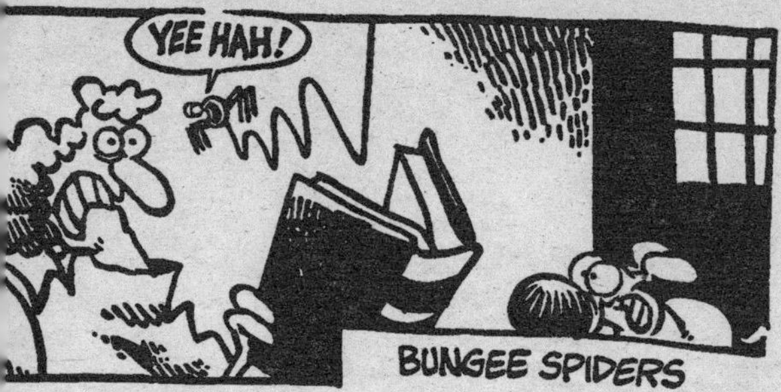
YEE HAH!

BUNGEE SPIDERS

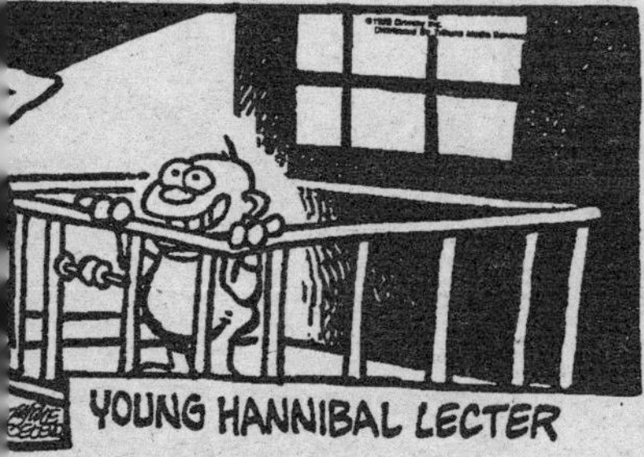

YOUNG HANNIBAL LECTER

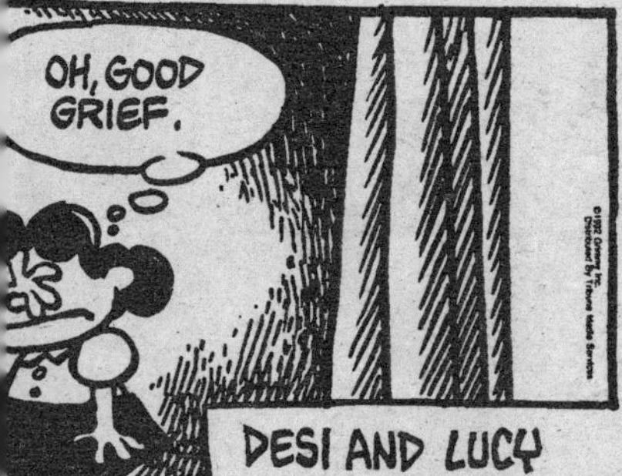
OH, GOOD GRIEF.

DESI AND LUCY

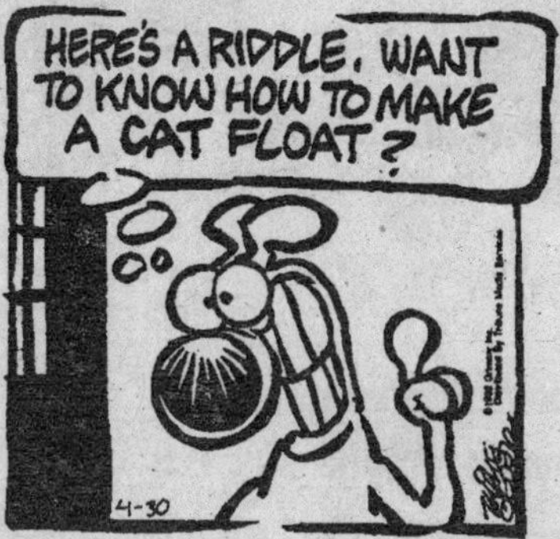
HERE'S A RIDDLE. WANT TO KNOW HOW TO MAKE A CAT FLOAT?
4-30

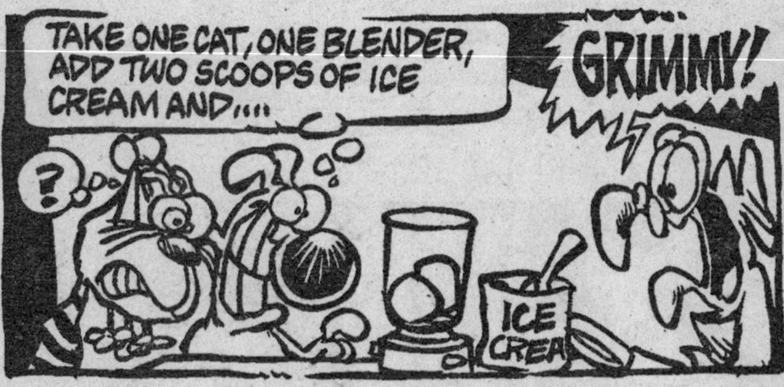
TAKE ONE CAT, ONE BLENDER, ADD TWO SCOOPS OF ICE CREAM AND....
GRIMMY!
?
ICE CREA

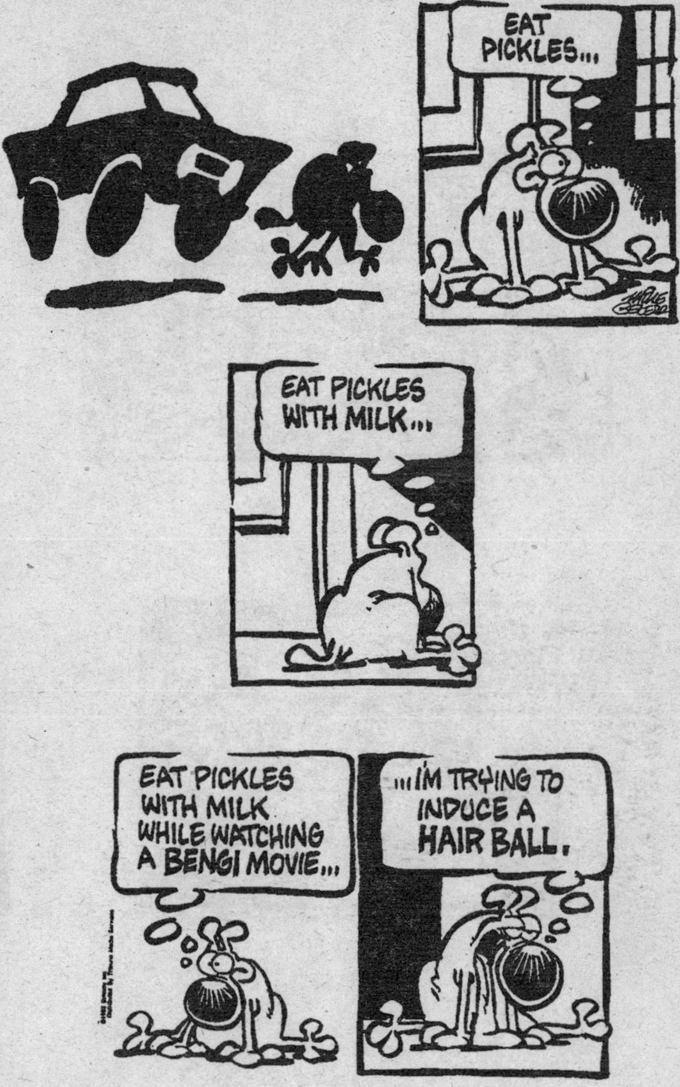
EAT PICKLES...
EAT PICKLES WITH MILK...
EAT PICKLES WITH MILK WHILE WATCHING A BENGI MOVIE...
...I'M TRYING TO INDUCE A HAIR BALL.

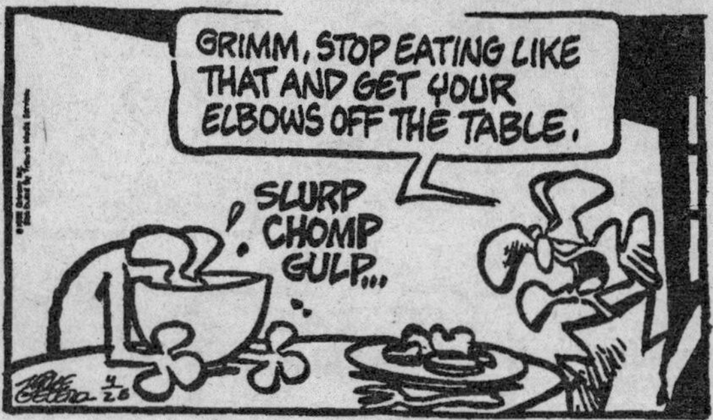
GRIMM, STOP EATING LIKE THAT AND GET YOUR ELBOWS OFF THE TABLE.
SLURP CHOMP GULP...

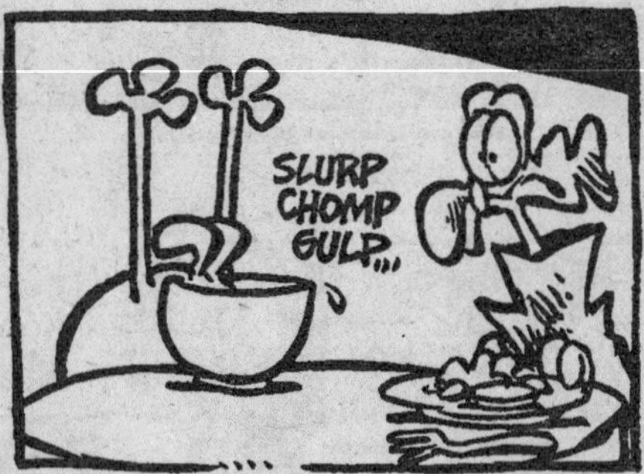
SLURP CHOMP GULP...
...

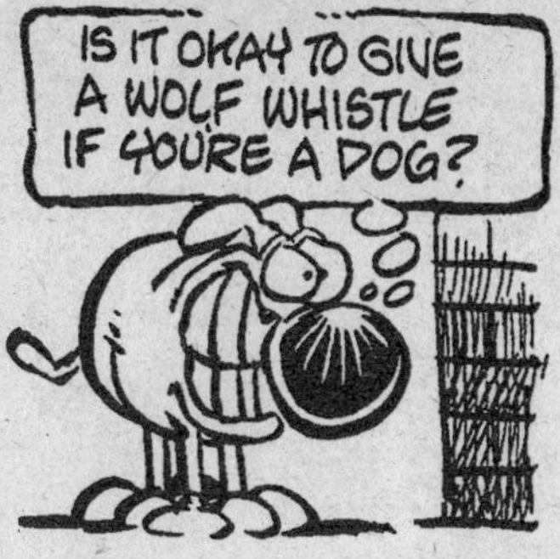
IS IT OKAY TO GIVE A WOLF WHISTLE IF YOU'RE A DOG?

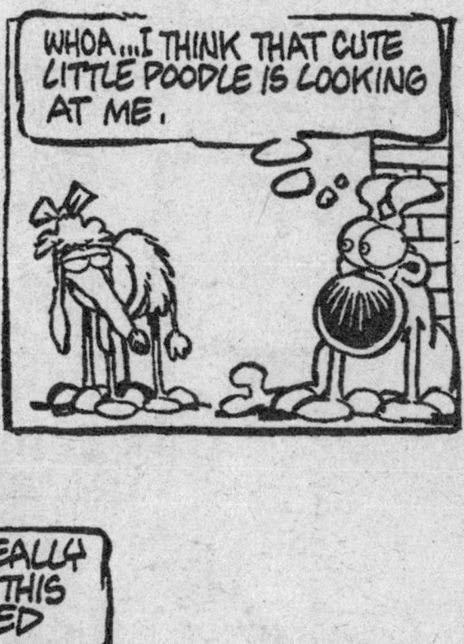
WHOA...I THINK THAT CUTE LITTLE POODLE IS LOOKING AT ME.

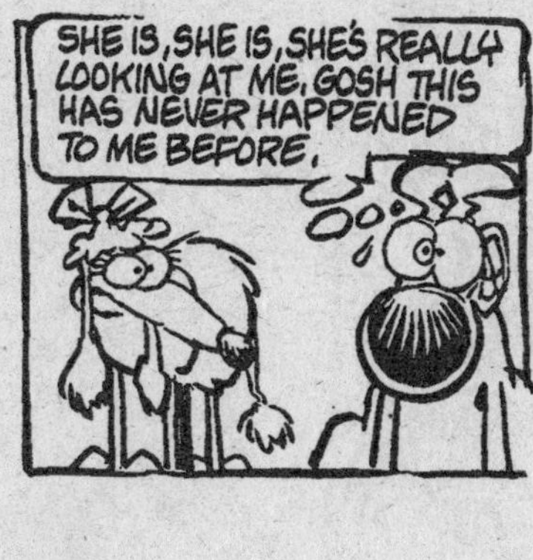
SHE IS, SHE IS, SHE'S REALLY LOOKING AT ME. GOSH THIS HAS NEVER HAPPENED TO ME BEFORE.

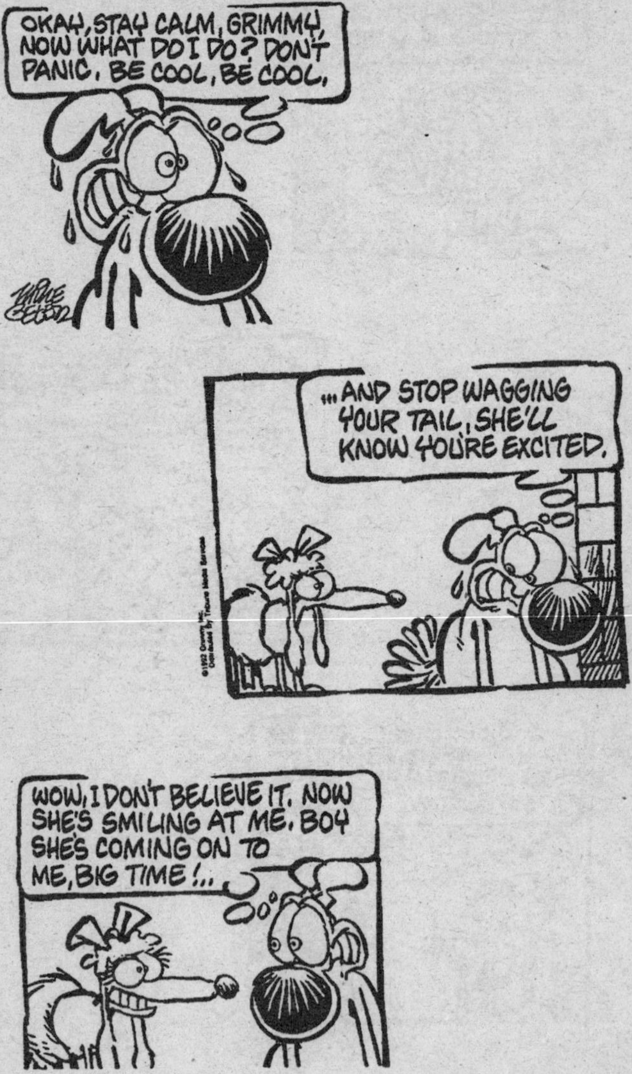
OKAY, STAY CALM, GRIMMY, NOW WHAT DO I DO? DON'T PANIC, BE COOL, BE COOL,
...AND STOP WAGGING YOUR TAIL, SHE'LL KNOW YOU'RE EXCITED.
WOW, I DON'T BELIEVE IT. NOW SHE'S SMILING AT ME. BOY SHE'S COMING ON TO ME, BIG TIME!...

OK, NOW WHAT WOULD TOM SELLECK DO? HE WOULD SMILE, LOOK RIGHT AT HER AND SAY SOMETHING ROMANTIC.

DID YOU KNOW YOU HAVE BEAUTIFUL EYES?

DID YOU KNOW YOU HAVE A GNAT CAUGHT IN YOUR NOSE HAIR?

I WANT TO DIE.

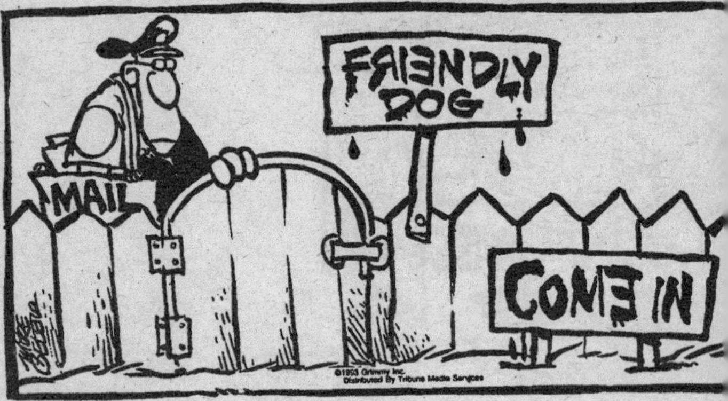
MAIL
FRIENDLY DOG
COME IN
©1993 Grimmy Inc.
Distributed By Tribune Media Services

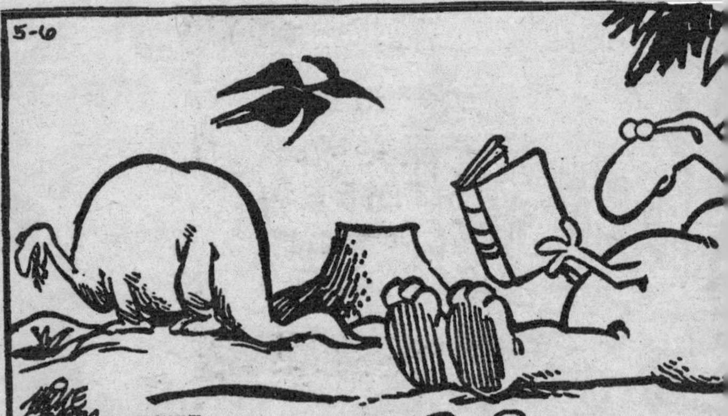
5-6

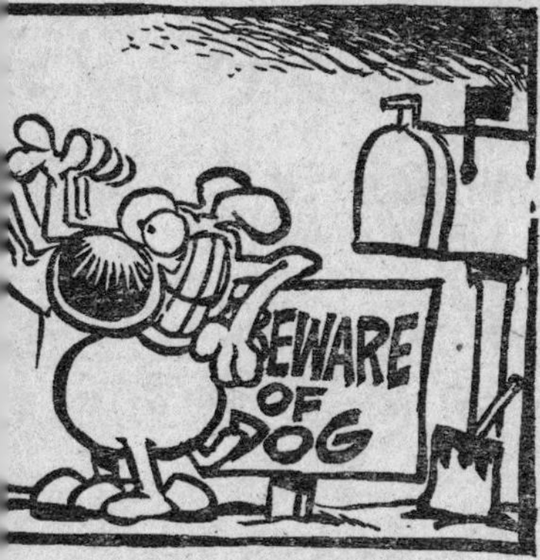
BEWARE
OF
DOG

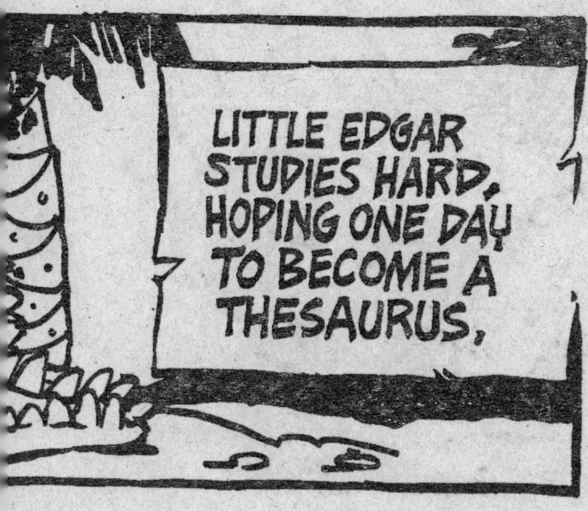
LITTLE EDGAR STUDIES HARD, HOPING ONE DAY TO BECOME A THESAURUS.

WHERE ARE THE GOODS

MANY OF OUR READERS ASK HOW THEY CAN BUY GRIMMY MERCHANDISE.

HERE IS A LIST OF LICENSEES IN THE UNITED STATES THAT CARRY GREAT STUFF!

GIVE THEM A CALL FOR YOUR LOCAL DISTRIBUTOR.

GRIMMY MERCHANDISE!!!

The Antioch Company
588 Dayton St.
Yellow Springs, OH 45387

PH 513/767-7379
Bookmarks, Wallet Cards,
"Largely Literary" products:
T-Shirts, Mugs, Journals, Pens,
Notepads, Bookplates, Bookmarks

C.T.I.
2160 North Pepper Rd.
Barrington, IL 60010

PH 800/284-5605
Balloons, Coffee Mugs

F.X. Schmid/USA
1 Industrial Way
Salem, NH 03079

PH 800/886-1236
Puzzles

Gibson Greetings
2100 Section Rd.
Cincinnati, OH 45237

PH 800/345-6521
Greeting Cards, Party
Papers, Gift Wrap etc...

Linda Jones Enterprises
17771 Mitchell
Irvine, CA 92714

PH 714/660-7791
Cels

Put Me On, Inc.
123 - 29th St. South
Birmingham, AL 35233

PH 800/466-8823
T-Shirts

Second Nature Software
1325 Officers' Row
Vancouver, WA 98661

PH 360/737-4170
Screen Saver Program

HTTP://WWW.GRIMMY.COM